British Impressionism

Nottingham Castle Museum

1989

Acknowledgements

*B*ritish Impressionism is a large exhibition which demands a great deal of work and enthusiasm from many people. In particular the staff at Nottingham Castle Museum would like to thank Dr Hilary Taylor, Art Historian who has put so much hard work, patience and dedication into the exhibition, into researching and selecting the works and into writing the catalogue. We are all very grateful to her. The exhibition would not have been possible without the generous co-operation of the lenders, both private owners and public institutions who have given freely of their time and effort.

Phillips Fine Art Auctioneers, London, have financially assisted the exhibition and allowed for such an ambitious catalogue. We are delighted that a large part of the exhibition will be on show at Phillips, 101 New Bond Street, London from 1–31 August 1989.

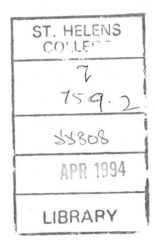

City of
Nottingham

Front cover: Detail from **The Red Shop** by W.R. Sickert
Courtesy of Norfolk Museums Service (Norwich Castle Museum).

The preview card for the exhibition is a detail from the picture **Kensington Gardens** by Paul Maitland
Courtesy of the Visitors of the Ashmolean Museum, Oxford.

Phillips are proud to sponsor this British Impressionism Exhibition, with paintings on loan from private and public collections all over the country, thus continuing our support to help fund important exhibitions.

The highly successful Painting in Newlyn exhibition which we supported in 1985 attracted over 250,000 visitors whilst our national tour has since helped to promote lesser known artists of the period through the salerooms.

This large exhibition reflects the influence of Whistler on his contemporaries, the response to French Impressionism and artistic activity in London, Cornwall and Glasgow during the 1880s and 1890s when artists were reacting vigorously to the staid conventions which dominated the British Academy and sharing with their French counterparts an enthusiasm for new ideas.

These paintings, including work by Stanhope Forbes, John Lavery and Sickert reflect an interest in everyday activities; the plein-air approach to painting outdoors and a portrayal of the English Countryside.

The exhibition provides a unique opportunity to view the richness and beauty of painting during this period.

Christopher Weston
Chairman and Chief Executive

Impressionism in Britain

*I*f the term 'Impressionism' is beset with contradictions when applied to French art during the second half of the nineteenth century, in a British context it embodies even more difficulties. In 1888 that staunch Victorian painter, W. P. Frith , was dismissive of a new and dangerous 'craze', Impressionism, which had "tainted the art of this country". Interestingly, Frith here seems to be referring particularly to the stylish black and white illustrations by journalistic artists like Charles Keene, the sort of work which was to be found in 'Punch' and several of the informative and entertaining magazines which proliferated at this time. He was also damning about the "occasional display of sooty flesh, and dingy, unmeaning–not to say unpleasant–subjects" and the "'nocturnes' and 'symphonies'" which seemed to him so fashionable. All of these Frith saw as the unpleasant and unfortunate consequence of "disease"; that mysterious affliction–of the brain, eye or hand–which recurs with such intriguing frequency in so much uncomprehending criticism of Impressionism.[1]

If Frith's was a fairly typical, establishment reaction to Impressionism, it was by no means the first time the subject had been discussed in the British press. Walter Hamilton, writing on 'The Aesthetic Movement in England' in 1882, displayed a similar, hapless confusion of terminology in his wholesale dismissal of "Pre-Raphaelite, or Aesthetic, or Impressionistic pictures", not one of which he deemed lively, healthy or natural.[2]

Others were more perceptive. Frederick Wedmore, in January 1883, succinctly summed up Impressionism as the evocation of modern life, the vivid expression of a personal response. He identified the main participants in the group as Degas, Renoir and Monet,[3] all of whom had been included in various exhibitions in London since the first small show organised by Durand-Ruel in 1870, when the dealer had encountered Monet and Pissarro in retreat from the Franco-Prussian war. A decade later, D.S.MacColl sensibly observed that in England the description was commonly applied to Whistler, Degas and Manet, as well as Monet and Pissarro.[4] What is interesting here is MacColl's clear recognition that 'Impressionism' was no simple label, but was a term conveniently applied to artists of varying character, whose work might be concerned with an urban or rural image, whose touch might be painterly or linear, whose colour might be brilliant or more sombre–but who shared something of the same excitement about the themes of modern life. MacColl, of course, had had the benefit of close contact with his fellow writer, George Moore. He, having enjoyed a Parisian 'vie de Bohème' in the 1870s, returned to London full of excitement about the new French school and full of particular admiration for Degas and Manet.

As already indicated, French Impressionist paintings were not unknown in Britain. Durand-Ruel, a dealer who devoted himself energetically to the cause, staged several Impressionist exhibitions in his gallery in Bond Street during the 1870s and early 1880s. More influential still were the large scale, plein-air paintings of peasants by Jules Bastien-Lepage, which were shown in London from 1880. Here were combined the fresh, pearly tones of French Impressionism with a decorative facture, and a poignant sentiment. **Pauvre Fauvette**, of 1881, for example, was a painting which made an appeal to personal and even political passion, expressed in a novel, painterly language. To a generation familiar with the social realism of artists such as Luke Fildes or Hubert Herkomer, increasingly conscious of a social and moral responsibility to the poor, and somewhat uneasy about the onslaught of urban and industrial growth, such paintings provided an entirely comprehensible version of Impressionism; a version which remained influential well into the new century.

Of all the commentaries on Impressionism to be found in British journals, perhaps the most persuasive and illuminating was actually one of the very first. This was published as early as 1876, only two years after the first exhibition in Paris of that rather diverse body of young painters who were soon to be dubbed 'Impressionist'. The French poet Stéphane Mallarmé, wrote in the 'Art Monthly Review' on 'The Impressionists and Edouard Manet'. The essay concludes with a simulated manifesto of the group and included amongst its adherents are Manet, Monet, Morisot, Renoir, Degas and Whistler:

That which I preserve through the power of Impressionism is not...any mere representation...but the delight of having recreated nature touch by touch...I content myself with reflecting on...that which perpetually lives yet dies every moment...an original and exact perception...(conveyed) with the steadfast gaze of a vision restored to its simplest perfection.[5]

This little essay, like so much of Mallarmé's work, is at once allusive and elusive. It depends–like the paintings he admired–upon evocation rather than mere description. There seems to have been little critical response to the article, which suggests that, of the few who read the essay, even fewer immediately comprehended it. Nevertheless in many ways it illuminates our understanding of British Impressionism, for Mallarmé here identified Impressionism as that search for an image of the everyday world, conveyed with an expression almost mystical in its individuality and sublime in its desire to snatch perfection from the jaws of change.

Thus it is that the great variety of British work which can be described as Impressionist, shares at least one preoccupation–a concern for the appearance of modern life; a concern sometimes heightened by the notion that intense personal experience and exquisite ephemeral appearance, could be combined in an image of immutable reality.

The Impact of Whistler

*I*t is, of course, significant that among the French exponents of Impressionism identified so far, there was another artist generally agreed to be one of the group, the expatriate American working in both London and Paris, James McNeill Whistler. His influence on radical British art during the last decades of the nineteenth century was enormous.

Whistler was an artist whose reception in British circles had been uncertain since he first settled in London in the late 1850s. Early success at the Royal Academy in 1860 with **At the Piano** was not isolated. **La Mère Gérard** in 1861, **The Coast of Brittany–Alone with the Tide** and **The Thames in Ice** in 1862, were amongst those paintings of Whistler's which were accepted and admired at the Royal Academy. His etchings, from the 1860s onwards, were also acclaimed. Interestingly, from a letter written by Manet, it seems that London, even as late as 1868, was regarded as a welcoming market-place by the young and ambitious artists of the 1860s.[6] Yet 1862 also witnessed Whistler's first rejection, when **The White Girl**, a painting into which much care and hope had been invested, was turned down by the Academy and then, in 1863, by the French Salon. For the next forty years, Whistler's work was the subject of much comment, both admiring and mocking. His own frequent letters to the press, his public 'Ten o'clock Lecture' in 1885, and

5

the edited publication of this material as 'The Gentle Art of Making Enemies' in June 1890, contributed much to the debate about his art.

Whister's uncertain fortunes of the 1860s and and 1870s culminated in melodrama. First, an opinionated Ruskin excoriated one of the paintings Whistler had submitted for show at the Grosvenor Gallery in May 1877; the painter sued the critic for libel. In December of the same year a French comedy was adapted for the Gaiety Theatre as 'The Grasshopper'. Its hero was Pygmalion Flippit, An Artist of the Future, whose appearance and mannerisms were clearly based on Whistler's. Indeed, the reference was made crystal clear when Flippit observed,

Like my great master, Whistler, I see things in a peculiar way, and I paint them as I see them. For instance, I see you a violet colour, and if I painted your portrait now I should paint it violet.[7]

In November 1878 Whistler's libel case finally came to trial. The scenes in the dock seem to have been more farcical even than those on the stage at the Gaiety. Whistler won his case and was awarded damages–the derisory sum of one farthing. He was in severe financial trouble. Not only did he have to sustain the costs of the action, but his new home, 'The White House', designed for him by E.W.Godwin, was also a strain upon his pocket. Furthermore, the steady stream of influential sitters, who had commissioned him to paint their portraits during the early 70s, had dried up. In 1879 Whistler was declared bankrupt. In September of that year he left London for Venice, with a small commission for twelve etchings from The Fine Art Society.

This was a turning point for Whistler. The exile in Venice–which was extended to over a year–cut him off from his circle of friends in London and from this time on he renewed his earlier links with Paris, establishing close ties with artists and writers. During the 1880s Whistler was in correspondence with both Monet and Degas; indeed, the former introduced Whistler to Mallarmé, who was to become one of his closest and most sympathetic friends. Furthermore, Manet–who died in 1883–was, clearly, an artist whom Whistler admired and he must also have been acquainted with Morisot; at her death in 1895 it was Mallarmé who was at her bedside.

The months in Venice were a turning point in other ways also. Here, Whistler established contact with many other younger artists studying in this venerated city. The painter had already had occasion to clarify and communicate his ideas when battling with the formidable Ruskin. Now he found himself surrounded by an admiring band who viewed him not only as a radical artist but also as an exciting teacher.

Interestingly, the character, subject matter and even the scale of Whistler's work changed during these months. The original twelve etchings proliferated, and on his return he had completed over fifty etchings and almost twice as many pastels. Without an established studio, he worked outside, on the street corners and in the doorways of the city–a city which, ironically, was for Whistler as exhilarating as it had been for Ruskin thirty years before. The tiny etchings and pastels produced during these months are infused with vigour, clarity and a marvellous sense of delight, characteristics which continued to flourish for the next twenty years. When the first twelve 'Etchings of Venice' were shown at The Fine Art Society in December 1880, that perspicacious French critic, Théodore Duret, noted their increased ease and simplification. He drew parallels with Impressionism in the lightness of touch, the grasp of momentary sensation, even the hint of mystery.[8] Early in 1883, fifty-one etchings, again mostly of Venice, were on show at The Fine Art Society. These also attracted considerable attention. One critic described Whistler as "eminently an 'Impressionist'...and one of the quickest and finest".[9]

Thus it was that when Whistler returned to England in 1880, he was evidently prepared–more vigorously than ever before–to take up the cause of radical art. Not only with his paintings, pastels, etchings and lithographs, but also in his approach to exhibitions, in his writings to the press and in the 'Ten o'clock Lecture', staged in 1885, he demanded that artists should question academic convention and defy insularity. Most particularly, he directed the attention of many young artists to developments across the Channel.

Whistler's return to England was celebrated by several successful exhibitions in the early 1880s. He began to attract the admiration of younger artists and writers in London. He became friendly with Oscar Wilde and Joseph Pennell, the etcher and future biographer, and in 1882 Walter

Sickert left the Slade to become Whistler's pupil and assistant. These were important years, for it is clear that Whistler was increasingly conscious of a need to articulate his ideas. The catalogues to his exhibitions were prefaced by comments and quotations. His one-man show at Dowdeswell's galleries in May 1884 was introduced by the determined assertion that "a picture is finished when all trace of the means used to bring about the end has disappeared"–a sharp attack on the contemporary association of artistic worth with manifest effort. It was early in the following year that Whistler's contribution to artistic debate reached its climax, when he delivered the extraordinary 'Ten o'clock Lecture', presented at that hour to eliminate the need for his audience to hasten from dinner.

It is easy to treat these writings as the amusing outpourings of a self-conscious, and sometimes scorned, artist, one renowned for his sharp tongue. Whistler was sufficiently perspicacious and tenacious to recognise that the role of art and artists, in the last part of the nineteenth century, was rapidly changing. New kinds of patronage reflected new social and economic patterns and demanded a very different kind of structural relationship between artists and society. Whistler was prepared to debate and communicate his ideas in public, despite his frequent and outspoken attacks on the philistinism of contemporary society. He took the Victorian passion for prosletysing into the arena of art. He had learned–from Ruskin, amongst others–that art had a public role of real importance. He rejected Ruskin's didactic and moral stance, but he was no less anxious to communicate and convince.

One of Whistler's most well-known observations comes from the 'Ten o'clock Lecture'. The lines have reverberated through the years and are worth quoting again:

Nature contains the elements, in colour and form, of all pictures, as the keyboard contains the notes of all music. But the artist is born to pick and choose, and group with science, these elements, that the result may be beautiful–as the musician gathers his notes, and forms his chords, until he brings forth from chaos glorious harmony. [10]

The emphasis upon scientific and musical method is fascinating. In conveying some understanding of art to a wider audience, Whistler shared Ruskin's need to relate it to another, more precise or familiar practice. For Ruskin the metaphor had been prosaic. Whistler rejected this out of hand; what had narrative or anecdote to do with art? For Whistler, the metaphor was a scientific or musical–sometimes even a poetic–one. Whereas painting was conventionally expected to offer a secure and reassuring reflection of reality, music lay at the emotional heart of many a Victorian existence, while science commanded the awe and respect of a society devoted to intellectual and material discovery. It is hard to overemphasise the extent to which Whistler's references must have demanded a radically new, and often alien, perception of the role and purpose of the visual arts–demands which still occasion debate today.

Throughout Whistler's writings of these later years there is a gathering frequency of reference to scientific method; a belief that persistent exploration and experimentation was vital to a greater understanding of the medium, the colour, the organisation, preparation and exhibition of a work of art. In 1898 he opened his 'Académie Carmen' in Paris and declared that his teaching was "based on proven scientific facts". Even accepting Whistler's taste for pithy remarks, there is no doubting the seriousness of his intentions. He insisted that students should learn from him a meticulous preparation of the colours on the palette, a consideration of the tones of the ground laid on a canvas, a concentrated approach which preceded any attempt to produce a painting.

Of course, 'scientific' method was being employed by artists outside England at this time and Whistler's investigations reflected those being undertaken across the Channel. Seurat's pointillist masterpiece, **La Grande Jatte**, for example, was shown with the radical exhibiting body, 'Les XX' in Brussels in 1887, a year in which Sickert had also been invited to exhibit. There can be no doubt that several artists in the Whistlerian circle must have known of this painting and become deeply interested in such experimental work. Nevertheless, it was only Whistler who so searchingly and deliberately attempted to reach some conclusions, not only about the technique and exhibition of his art, but also about its role and purpose in society.

Many of Whistler's followers were influenced by his exploratory methods. Some merely adopted his mannerisms–perhaps inevitably so, given the 'master's' preoccupation with an elegant appearance and absolute statement. These, who responded only to the superficial and idiosyncratic appearance of things, were dismissed with short shrift. Mortimer Menpes, although one of the early admirers, was ridiculed as a circus entertainer. Oscar Wilde, who travelled extensively in America, lecturing on the seriousness of artistic endeavour, was caricatured by Whistler for his eccentric dress and manners. It is in the interesting experiments of another of his followers, Theodore Roussel, that a more substantial response to Whistler's influence is found. He was described as "a mathematician and a poet", fascinated by all sorts of experiment, particularly in relation to what he termed "chromatic analysis". In his studio at his death there were numerous small squares of paper, coloured in various shades of one hue; an indication of his preoccupation with research into the problems of purity of optical tone.

The Royal Society of British Artists

*T*he 1880s and '90s saw Whistler not only active as a teacher but very busy participating in and organizing various exhibiting bodies. In 1884 he was elected a member of the rather insignificant Society of British Artists, based in Suffolk Street. By June 1886, with the staunch support of admirers such as William Stott of Oldham, he had been elected President and a year later the group received a Royal Charter. The Royal Society of British Artists was thus one of the first sites of Whistler's activities in the realms of exhibition organization. Again, it is clear that he was acutely conscious of the impact of the expanding body of urban middle classes on the nature and purpose of the art exhibition. He was aggressively critical of the crude commercialism of the art market-place and yet very much aware of the necessity for exhibition. What he required was that the presentation of art should reflect something of the personality of the individual pictures and should also speak of the dignity of the practice. Ornate, crowded exhibitions–as depicted in Frith's paintings of the Royal Academy in 1881–merely contributed to the sensation of art as a commodity, the product of whim and greed. Whistler embarked on something much more exhilarating and poetic.

Already, in the early 1880s, in the exhibitions organized at The Fine Art Society and Dowdeswell's, Whistler had devoted attention to the simple decoration of the gallery. From France, Camille Pissarro wrote to his son, Lucien, then in London, that he very much regretted not being able to see Whistler's show at The Fine Art Society in 1883, "as much for the fine dry points as for the setting, which for Whistler has so much importance".[11]

At the R.S.B.A. Whistler took advantage of his new position with an autocracy worthy of Ruskin:

But no sooner was he seated in the Presidential chair,
Than he changed our exultations into wailings of despair
For he broke up our traditions and went in for foreign schools
Turning out the work we're noted for and making us look fools.[12]

He first determined upon a radical simplification of presentation. In 1888 he designed a velarium for use in the exhibitions, to ensure a subtle and diffused light. He refused to allow the walls to be crowded with paintings, insisting instead that each piece should be carefully and spaciously sited. Perhaps it was inevitable that uproar followed; hard-pressed artists, familiar with the customary careless overcrowding of canvases, feared for their livelihood. Empty space upon the wall was calculated in £.s.d. The consequence followed within a short time. In June, amid some acrimony, Whistler resigned as president of the R.S.B.A. and a number of his close associates, including Walter Sickert and Theodore Roussel, followed his example. As usual, Whistler summed up the situation: "The Artists have come out; the British remain".[13]

The New English Art Club

*W*histler had lost the opportunity to lead an important exhibiting body. His immediate reaction was to turn to another, new group, established specifically to promote and show the work of younger and more radical artists, the New English Art Club. Whistler's work was on show in

Brussels, Paris and Munich in 1888, but it is clear, nevertheless, that he still hoped to influence the future of British art. Founded in 1886, under the guidance of Fred Brown, W.J.Laidlay, Francis Bate–together with others who were quite closely associated with Whistler and also very much preoccupied with developments in French art–the main purpose of the N.E.A.C. was to provide an alternative to the Academy and Suffolk Street. It certainly became one of the most important sites of exhibition, particularly for those young artists recently emerged from a spell in one of the free academies in Paris or, a little later, the Slade and the tutorship of Fred Brown.

To go to Paris to study was the aim of many young painters at this time. There they searched for freedom, both social and artistic. Paris was seen as an escape from the pressure to conform. The training available at the Royal Academy was derided by one young artist, who described the "paralysing degree of finish" which was required of a drawing and the "slick surface smoothness" which was a "standard of excellence" in a painting.[14] But France offered more than just a different, less rigid style of teaching. It offered challenge and excitement in artistic, political and social spheres; indeed, these were not separate fields of activity, but were intimately related, one to the other. Furthermore, beyond the enchanting prospect of Paris, there was the vast, unspoilt, unfamiliar countryside, with inhabitants and customs which offered an image of that purer, more primitive existence which otherwise only survived in England in the medieval fantasies inspired by the Pre-Raphaelites and the Arts and Crafts Movement.

Once back in England, these young artists planned to organize an exhibiting body which would import some of the freedom they had enjoyed across the Channel. Stylistically, they were committed to the vigour and individuality characteristic of French work–whether Realist, Naturalist or Impressionist–while politically the debate centred on how best to establish and run a group which was manifestly democratic in its structure.

It is clear that from the outset, there was no absolute unanimity of aim amongst those who exhibited with the Club. Indeed, when Frederick Leighton, the President of the Royal Academy, described the artists as "impressionists" after visiting the first show, W.J.Laidlay reacted against this unfairness, "for we were anything but of one school".[15]

Nevertheless, it was apparently clear to all that the new group represented an important step away from the customary insularity of British art. That eminently reasonable critic, P.G.Hamerton, carefully summed it up when he observed that perhaps "it would be accurate enough to say that the pictures nearly all show signs of the influence of the modern French school".[16]

The first exhibition of the N.E.A.C. was held at the Marlborough Galleries and was dominated by the kind of rustic naturalism which owed much to Bastien-Lepage and to the English social realists such as Herkomer. It was from the following year, when the group was enlarged and moved to the Dudley Gallery, that a more substantial number of Whistler's adherents could be found exhibiting. By 1888, the Club included not only Whistler himself but also others who had left the R.S.B.A.; Walter Sickert, Theodore Roussel, the reclusive Paul Maitland and Philip Wilson Steer amongst them. There were other groups, too. From Glasgow came a contingent of artists, the majority of whom had studied in France, including John Lavery, James Guthrie and Edward Walton. From the remoteness of Newlyn, on the Cornish coast, artists such as Stanhope Forbes, Henry Tuke and Norman Garstin submitted work. The following year Whistler's fellow countryman, John Singer Sargent, having made a pilgrimage to meet Monet in Giverny, exhibited for the first time. By 1892, those young artists who had studied under Fred Brown became dominant, amongst them Alfred Thornton and the intriguing Arthur Studd.

It was in 1893 that Fred Brown–one of the moving forces in the N.E.A.C. since its inception–took over as Professor at the Slade School of Art. He replaced the ageing Alphonse Legros and immediately directed his students' attention to France, where he believed they would find something of the vigour and expressiveness he wished to promote. In London, the N.E.A.C. came increasingly to be identified with the Slade and for many of the rising stars trained under Brown, the New English became a second home.

Whistler's own attachment to the N.E.A.C. was short lived. After 1889 he did not exhibit there again. Yet his presence was still felt by many. It is interesting to find that, almost a decade later, his name was still revered at the Slade. Augustus John, in his autobiography, recalled the thrill of excitement which went through the school when the celebrated figure of the master was spied one day in 1896.[17] Certainly, the elegant portrait of John, painted by another young Slade student, William Orpen, and shown at the N.E.A.C. in the summer of 1900, demonstrates the admiration of both artist and sitter, for it pays clear tribute to Whistler's portrait of Carlyle, acquired by Glasgow Corporation in 1891.

The London Impressionists

*I*t is evident that, from the beginning, the New English Art Club was the scene of much discussion and not a little disagreement. In 1889 Sickert wrote to that elegant Anglophile, Jacques-Emile Blanche, that he felt it better to stay in the background that year, as the dominating faction at the N.E.A.C., "whose touch is square and who all paint alike", was increasingly antagonistic towards the "impressionist nucleus". It is interesting that Sickert was here distinguishing himself from that group headed by George Clausen, the Newlyn School and others initiated into the style of Bastien-Lepage. Sickert's own allegiance was directly to Whistler and the French Impressionist art to which Whistler had introduced him. Since his trip to Paris in 1883, when he had accompanied Whistler's **Arrangement in Grey and Black: Portrait of the Painter's Mother** to the Salon, Sickert had been familiar with the work of the Impressionists, particularly Manet, Degas and Monet. The summer of 1885 was the first of many Sickert spent on the coast near Dieppe, in the company of Whistler, Degas, Monet and J.E.Blanche. Obviously, Sickert had a fairly sophisticated understanding of the various debates surrounding the Impressionists. He shared Degas' fascination with the theatre and, during the late 1880s, visited the music halls regularly, night after night. Nevertheless, Sickert jealously defended the attractions of London rather than Paris. When it was suggested that the inspiration for his subject matter must have come from France, he reacted with irritation.

It is surely unnecessary to go so far afield as Paris to find an explanation of the fact that a Londoner should seek to render on canvas a familiar and striking scene, in the midst of the town in which he lives...the fact that the painter sees in any scene the elements of pictorial beauty is the obvious and sufficient explanation of his motive for painting it.[18]

This preoccupation with London was important and it heralds a growing critical awareness that 'Impressionism' in England meant something different from 'Impressionism' in France. These were the years when Whistler and his associates were wandering around the streets of the capital, selecting little shops and street corners to portray on small, wooden panels, or etch onto a plate. It was a devotion maintained at a time when Paris was increasingly being regarded as the artistic capital, especially in 1889, the year of the Exposition Universelle. Thus, when Sickert and some of his associates decided to hold an exhibition in that same year, it was with very deliberate intent that they called themselves 'London Impressionists'; an interesting sign of maturing independence from France.

This exhibition, staged at the Goupil Gallery in December, included the work of ten artists, all of whom were rather disillusioned with the New English Art Club. Besides Sickert, their number comprised Philip Wilson Steer, Sidney Starr, Francis James, George Thomson, Bernhard Sickert, Fred Brown, Francis Bate, Theodore Roussel and Paul Maitland. They showed seventy paintings, various in theme, scale and style; but they had in common a professed interest in contemporary French painting, a preoccupation with their own capital city, the English landscape and coastal haunts, and, perhaps above all, a shared admiration for Whistler.

The preface to the catalogue of the London Impressionist exhibition was written by Walter Sickert. It is easy to find the text somewhat confused, and even naive, in parts. Yet this is probably because Sickert actually did understand just how tenuous were the links which connected together the very various work of those described as 'Impressionist'. He recognised that it was impossible quickly to sum up a list of qualifying characteristics. He devoted himself, instead, to conveying something of his own perception of a work of art, in words which echo those of Whistler:

Impressionism as understood by its votaries...accepts as the aim of the painter what Edgar Allen Poe asserts to be the sole legitimate province of the poem, beauty...[19]

The religious reverberations of "votaries", the evocation of the mysterious writings of Poe, the dedication to the poetic; it becomes clear that Sickert, far from floundering, was selecting his words with exquisite care. There is much here that could be compared not only to Whistler, but also to Mallarmé's definition of Impressionism published thirteen years earlier. Art, Sickert declared, was a precious and tenuous thing, a matter of "temperament...education and experience", concerned with the "production of...emotion induced by the complex phenomenon of vision". For these artists, painting was not about anecdote, nor even about realism. They had "no wish to record anything merely because it exists". They declared themselves, "strong in the belief that for those who live in the most wonderful and complex city in the world, the most fruitful course of study lies in a persistent effort to render the magic and poetry which they daily see around them..."[20]

When this little essay is placed in the context of contemporary debate about the nature of Impressionism, it becomes even more illuminating. Sickert's emphasis upon preciousness, education, experience and complexity, introduces the image of an artist who is the exact antithesis of the 'Impressionist' so often characterised—and even caricatured—in much British press comment about the new French art. If Edward Armitage, an academic painter, visiting Paris in 1887, could refer to the "high priests of the new creed" as "more childishly absurd than ever" in their uncouthness, lunacy, decadence and charlatanism, Sickert and his fellow English "votaries" were obviously prepared to debate the issue.[21]

Newlyn

*I*t is very probable that Sickert's London Impressionists were emphasising their attachment to the metropolis not only in order to distinguish themselves from their French counterparts, but also to express their disdain for those who had discovered retreats in distant corners of Britain.

In both England and France the myth of a purer, more primitive way of life was a persuasive one. In each case it was a myth fostered by political belief and social expediency. Instability, industrial squalor, cultural uncertainty, could all be viewed and criticised from the security of a commitment to the past, to the peasant, to the cottage—to a rural arcadia. Furthermore, the wide open spaces seemed to offer an opportunity for personal expression which was inhibited by the busy and conformist demands of urban life. Thus, in France, the Impressionists were predominantly concerned with painting in the countryside or along the coast. Those, like Degas, who chose to stay in the city did so in the full consciousness of the kind of statement they were making; and it is not insignificant that they so often concentrated on places of entertainment,—emblems of superficiality, greed and materialism, as well as of comfort and convenience.

From the middle of the century in France, artists had left the city behind and had gathered in remote corners of the countryside. Many of these young British artists studying in Paris joined with Americans, Scandinavians and others, spending their summers in such communities, emulating Jean-François Millet and successors such as Bastien-Lepage. The regional attractions of Normandy and Brittany were particularly strong. Only recently opened up by improved communications, these were areas where the tourist was promised a taste of the real France. The young Stanhope Forbes joined his friend H.H.La Thangue on the first of several trips to Brittany in 1881. The two immediately set to work 'en plein air' struggling with the demands of changing light and weather. Such difficulties, such devotion to an immediate response to the outside world, were revelled in and were regarded as part of the necessary attributes of modern painting, expressive of honesty, democracy and serious endeavour.

So great was this preoccupation with struggle, with the need to master all sorts of difficulties, that the artists sometimes felt obliged to work in the most exceptionally demanding circumstances. This introduces another of the strands of contemporary argument about the quality of Impressionism. Scientific observation, dedication, reverence for nature and sheer masculine strength were all thus celebrated, and offered a rebuttal to the notion of the effete, careless, self-indulgent bohemian revelling in notoriety. It is interesting that when the critic D.S.MacColl began to defend the work of the French Impressionists in the English press, he stressed the scientific, experimental nature of Monet's investigations.[22] Ironically, in later years, Monet evidently felt some irritation with the fact that the dogma of painting 'en plein air' had become more persuasive than the results.[23]

Stanhope Forbes, on his return to England, discovered again the attractions of the countryside, when he arrived in the Cornish fishing village of Newlyn early in 1884. There he found the Birmingham artist, Walter Langley, amongst a small group already settled. Forbes, shortly followed by friends who included Henry Tuke, Frank Bramley and T.C.Gotch, noted that "artists were flocking in here each day".[24]

The artists of Newlyn soon established a common bond and were identified by the press as Impressionist. They devoted themselves to substantial images of rural activities, often painted out of doors, sometimes under difficult circumstances. They submitted to London exhibitions, including, of course, the N.E.A.C., and they showed, too, in the provinces. In Nottingham, for example, the Castle Museum staged a 'Special Exhibition of Paintings by Cornish Painters' in 1894, from which a number of works were bought for the collection.

There is no doubt that the hero of this group of artists was not Monet, nor even Degas; still less was it Whistler. The reputation of Bastien-Lepage had reached new heights after his death in 1884. His characteristically broad, square brushstroke, the cool tones, the abrupt presentation of figures,–these were taken up as the hallmarks of the Newlyn School. The work was perceived as being objectively naturalistic, the painter's eye almost photographic in its unflinching response to the world. This deliberate rejection of personal expression was, perhaps, the most distinctive feature of the Newlyners. Together with the retreat (partial at least) from urban sophistication, the celebration of the physical difficulties of plein-air painting, the devotion to sharp, blond tones, this self-abnegation was a mark of democratic, puritan honesty.

Such reforming zeal inevitably leads to conflict, and it was the art of Whistler, Sickert and their circle that Stanhope Forbes particularly rejected. He described his "contempt" for these artists in strong terms, which can only be understood in the context of the almost religious nature of the debate.[25] Forbes was suspicious of Whistler and his 'votaries', with their dedication to the expression of subtle and exquisite responses to the natural world; the Newlyners advocated honest, impersonal objectivity. This was an important difference. It reflected, to some extent, debates that were also in progress in France. But in England, where the Reformation provided the back-drop to the very real religious anxieties and suspicions of these years, the social and spiritual– as well as artistic–significance of the argument cannot be underestimated.

Staithes

Newlyners may well have congratulated themselves on their dedication and simplicity; there is no doubt, however, that their adopted home often appears in the paintings of its devotees as a place where peace, comfort and even plenty accompanied the hard work of the native inhabitants. Staithes, on the North Yorkshire coast near Whitby, was altogether more harsh, demanding and difficult. Here, indeed, the life of a painter was anything but soft. Frederick Jackson, Dame Laura Knight and Harold Knight were amongst the central figures of the group which established itself on this remote coast during the closing years of the nineteenth century.

Like so many who were dubbed 'Impressionist' by the English press, several of the Staithes group also studied in Paris. Jackson, for example, was in Paris at the same time as fellow north-countrymen, Edward Stott, William Stott of Oldham, and others such as H.H.La Thangue. He also shared with these artists a fascination for large pictures, where plein-air observation–pursued in all weathers–was combined with a reverent approach to the mysticism of nature.

It is interesting, in passing, to observe the fact that both Newlyn and Staithes were villages where the local economy depended upon the sea and fishing. The appeal of remote, rural retreats in an age increasingly obsessed by large scale, industrial and urban concerns, has already been noted. Fishing villages were, however, more than just picturesque. Here, life depended upon the sea and the elements, with all their vagaries, rich harvests and hardship. The sea itself signified the history and character of an island nation and it is no coincidence that it frequently provided a theme for painters during these years.

Glasgow

*T*he New English Art Club, in its early years, included the work of yet another distinctive group, the majority of whom issued not from remote country villages at all, but from the busy city of Glasgow. The reasons for this apparently sudden burst of cultural activity in Glasgow are several, but must depend partly on the rich business life of the city. A number of excellent private collections of contemporary painting, especially of French and Dutch schools, were being built up. Amongst the dealers, Alexander Reid stood out as one of the most independent and adventurous. He bought and exhibited in London and Scotland works by French Impressionists and Whistler, as well as other, more conventional pieces. Before long he was buying the work of the Glasgow School.[26]

The young artists from Glasgow included Edward Walton, Joseph Crawhall, James Guthrie and George Henry. John Lavery was also an important associate and almost all of them, in one way or another, were enthralled by the idea of France; the stimulating training to be found in Paris, the unconventional freedom offered by its rural retreats. Like the artists from Newlyn, they had a great admiration for the subject matter and style of Bastien-Lepage, but unlike their southern colleagues, they did not find this incompatible with a deep admiration for Whistler. A contemporary critic observed in 1894 that "the most powerful individual factor in the formulation of their artistic aims and technical methods has been the genius of Mr Whistler".[27]

It is significant, of course, that artists from Glasgow enjoyed a much less insular cultural tradition than those in southern England. They had the confidence to admire many different kinds of artistic practice and to take Europe by storm when they were invited to show at the International Exhibition in Munich, in 1890. This confirmed the standing of the group shortly after they had first exhibited together in London, at the New English Art Club in 1887. By 1890 they had a large showing at the N.E.A.C., displayed their work in an 'Impressionist Room' at the Glasgow Institute, and enjoyed a critical success at the Grosvenor Gallery, before the presentation of no fewer than sixty paintings and drawings at Munich.

The confidence of these artists was also instrumental in their founding of 'The Scottish Art Review' in 1888. The magazine publicised the work not only of the Glasgow School but also that of Constable, Corot, Stott of Oldham, Puvis de Chavannes, Burne Jones and, of course, Whistler. The slightest of glances at the work of these painters admired by the Glasgow School illuminates their own aims and ambitions; precision and deftness of touch, a subtle understanding of tone, an empathetic response to the subject matter. What they most valued was simply described by a contemporary writer; "personal emotion, expressed in an impressionistic manner and on a decorative basis".[28]

Robert Macaulay Stevenson was probably the most significant critic on 'The Scottish Art Review'. In 1895 he published an important book on Velasquez which offers great insight into yet another interpretation of Impressionism found on these shores. Several painters and critics, attempting to promote radical art, made unflinching references to the work of predecessors venerated by tradition. This was in an attempt to engage with the notion that the anarchic Impressionists not only rejected, but even derided tradition. Thus Giorgione and Titian, Delacroix and Corot, and— even better—Constable and Turner, were all introduced as the antecedents of Impressionism. Stevenson's serious analysis of Velasquez is perhaps the most sustained contribution to this debate.

The art of Spain had exerted considerable appeal, in both France and England, at least since the 1860s; it is an appeal which is clearly reflected in the work of Manet and Whistler at this time. As early as 1862 Whistler had been planning a trip to Madrid, to see the Velasquez paintings in the Prado. In the event, he never reached Madrid, but there are numerous accounts of Whistler's continuing admiration for the Spanish master. During the 1890s Stevenson frequented the same circles as Whistler. Indeed, in his introduction to the book, Stevenson wrote that the "sympathetic comprehension of a Whistler or a Carolus-Duran is needed for Madrid".[29]

The closing chapter of 'Velasquez' is devoted to 'The Lesson of Impressionism'. Although Stevenson acknowledges that "many people, in speaking of impressionism, imply that it must be unmodelled, scarce drawn, roughly surfaced, ugly, at least commonplace in subject", he suggests that the "work of Velasquez should be sufficient evidence to persuade them that they misunderstand the question".[30]

It is clear that Stevenson offers here a model of Impressionism which "allows many and divers" approaches. Essentially, however, he applauded the subtle command of tone and the wonderful "running, slippery touch" of Velasquez. There can be no doubt that this offered a persuasive model to many of the painters working, and exploring new ideas, in Glasgow.

Glasgow was home, even though some members of the School spent their summers working in the countryside–for pleasure rather than principle. It was perhaps inevitable, however, that the attractions of London lured several of them away from Scotland. Certainly, a number spent at least some of their working life in the English capital, often, in the 1890s, in close contact with Whistler. Yet this was not before Walton, assisted by Guthrie and the others, had successfully petitioned the Glasgow Corporation to acquire, in 1891, Whistler's **Portrait of Thomas Carlyle** for the city.

The International Society of Sculptors, Painters and Gravers

It has already been indicated that, during these years, there was no shortage of French Impressionist paintings on display in London. Particularly from the later 1880s Durand-Ruel, Goupil and other dealers organised Impressionist exhibitions, and often included works by Whistler. At the latter's invitation, Monet submitted four pieces to the R.S.B.A. in the winter of 1887. In the following year the N.E.A.C., for the first of many times, included an Impressionist work, a pastel by Degas. Thus it can be no surprise that in May 1898, at the opening show of the International Society, of which Whistler was President, there was work by Manet, Degas, Monet, Sisley, Renoir and other artists from abroad.

The first Council Meeting of the International Society was held at Prince's Skating Rink, Knightsbridge, in December 1897. The report of this meeting reveals Whistler's absence, but also the fact that plans for a major exhibition were already well in hand. There can be no doubt that Whistler was closely involved with the organization of this ambitious Society and that it was he who promoted the desire to establish closer links with artists from many countries.

There was a strong Scottish contingent supporting Whistler. E.A. Walton, who had left Glasgow and become a neighbour at Cheyne Walk in 1893, was active in the initial stages, while John Lavery was the Vice-President of the Society. The International Exhibitions were organized under Whistler's presidency until his death in 1903 and, although he was spending much of his time in Paris, his ultimate control of the progress of the exhibitions was never in doubt, for there was an unbroken correspondence between himself and other members of the committee and he insisted that all decisions should be sent to him for ratification.

Whistler was very keen from the first to display much foreign work, and was particularly anxious that French art should be well represented. Durand-Ruel promised paintings by Degas, Manet and Monet, though Degas himself, now something of a recluse, resented being disturbed over the exhibition.[31] Quite possibly, he was not prepared to witness a repeat of the extraordinary debates which had followed the showing of **Au Café**, then retitled **L'Absinthe**, at the opening exhibition of the Grafton Galleries in February 1893. D.S. MacColl, in the 'Spectator', had declared that "'L'Absinthe', by Degas, is the inexhaustible picture, the one that draws you back, and back again", and had condemned those who were repulsed by it to "confusion and affliction". Nevertheless, many were indeed repulsed, and they did not hesitate to express their feelings; the battle raged on in the press for much of the rest of the year.[32]

Degas showed six pieces, including three pastels of **Dancers** at this first exhibition of the International Society. Perhaps the most substantial French painting to be shown was, however, by Manet. His **Execution of the Emperor Maximilian** was a painting Whistler was delighted to secure, and it certainly attracted considerable attention. True, it was not an Impressionist painting. Indeed, it was described as "one of the finest pieces of historical painting of the century". Yet it was also recognised, and admired, as the work of a remarkable pioneer.[33]

Whistler himself contributed nine major works, of all periods, to the International in 1898; a sign that, for him, the Society represented the culmination of his career. In the following years the exhbitions included numerous Impressionist paintings by Monet, Degas, Pissarro, Sisley and Renoir, and an increasingly ambitious selection of work from many countries. Indeed, several shows were arranged abroad, in America and Germany. Here too, Whistler chose to show some of his own most splendid paintings and in 1905, after his death two years earlier, the Society organized a major and highly acclaimed retrospective exhibition of the work of its former President.

British Art at the Turn of the Century

*I*t is clear that by the turn of the century there was in Britain, as well as elsewhere in Europe and America, a fairly extensive familiarity with the work of the French Impressionists, other 'plein-air' painters and with that of the charismatic American, James McNeill Whistler. Indeed, for many on this side of the Channel - even young artists and aspiring radicals - no very clear distinction existed between the different kinds of painting which were dubbed Impressionist. The critic, Frank Rutter, later noted that in the 1890s the "'impressionism' of Whistler and Velasquez, which meant seeing a scene broadly.... and enveloping it in air and light" was little differentiated from the "'impressionism'... of Monet and Renoir which further meant analysing the colour in shadows and ruling out all neutral tints".[34] He concluded with the wry observation that those who admired Whistler and those who did not, similarly adopted the word 'impressionism' as a kind of convenience label identifying all the work about which they felt most strongly. 'Impressionism' signified the arena of battle.

The year 1905 was an important one, for not only was there a major exhibition of the work of Whistler, but also a magnificent display of 315 French Impressionist paintings in a show organised at the Grafton Galleries by Durand-Ruel. Frank Rutter described the "overwhelming" impact of this exhibition, which included examples of French Impressionism "from its earliest beginnings, through the masterpieces of its maturity, to its culminating achievements":

Never before...had we seen Nature painted in all the prismatic radiance of summer sunshine. These pictures sparkled, they scintillated with light...with dancing pinpoints of a myriad hues.[35]

The paintings certainly did arouse the enthusiasm of those "in sympathy with their technique"– but these were definitely still in the minority. Rutter himself worked hard, with the support of colleagues such as Sargent, Lavery and D.S MacColl, to organise a subscription to purchase an Impressionist painting for the National Gallery. He declared that he wanted to buy Monet's **Vétheuil: Sunshine and Snow.** In the end, however, because these French artists "had not been dead long enough for England", Rutter–and the nation–had to be satisfied with a Boudin.[36]

There can be no doubt that the opportunity afforded by the presentation of these two major shows in 1905, contributed to a growing awareness of the differences between English and French Impressionism–at least for those who were interested in making such analyses. At the beginning of the year, Laurence Housman wrote a perceptive article entitled 'Two Kinds of Impressionism'.

"English Impressionism", he observed, "may be said to deal with the tone-values far more than with problems of colour"; for the French, colour was paramount.[37]

Indeed, among the reasons for continuing public nervousness about these new-fangled ideas was the growing suspicion that they were, in origin, foreign; worse they were French. It was bad enough that Whistler was an American–and apparently proud of it–but the fact that so many young British artists looked to France could scarcely be tolerated. Even in the early years of the twentieth century, British suspicion of French culture had not recovered from the horror and threat sparked off by the Revolution more than one hundred years earlier. The British establishment well understood that the unconventional art of the Impressionists and their successors offered a challenge to the stability of the social order. As early as 1861 Lady Eastlake, the wife of the Director of the National Gallery, had feared that "French art is now of a class in which neither the most enlightened, nor the most indulgent eye can take pleasure...such (an) exhibition...goes far to ruin art for half a generation".[38]

The early years of the new century witnessed the publication of a considerable number of articles and books dealing with Impressionism. D.S. MacColl's 'Nineteenth Century Art' was followed by Camille Mauclair's 'The French Impressionists 1860-1900' in 1903, and Wynford Dewhurst's 'Impressionist Painting, Its Genesis and Development' in 1904. Each of these volumes reveals an interesting preoccupation with the national characteristics of Impressionism. While Mauclair insisted that the new art was not "a violent denial of the French traditions, but nothing more or less than a logical return to the very spirit of these traditions",[39] Dewhurst, himself an English Impressionist painter, was determined that,

Impressionism owes its birth to Constable; and its ultimate glory, the works of Claude Monet, is profoundly inspired by the works of Turner.[40]

Xenophobia was only partially calmed by such reassurances.

Nevertheless, despite continued public uncertainty, the early years of the new century witnessed a growing number of artists who were travelling widely, reviewing the art of their neighbours with interest, and contributing to the new, independent exhibiting groups which were flourishing. The Allied Artists' Association was established by Frank Rutter in 1908; Sickert's studios in Fitzroy Street became a gathering-place for some young artists who formed the Camden Town Group in 1911; the Carfax Gallery was one of several dealers' galleries to show new work. The New English Art Club, the International Society and several enormous and official international exhibitions continued to display a wide range of work. This busy activity culminated in 1910 and 1912 when Roger Fry organized two major displays of Impressionist and Post-Impressionist work at the Grafton Galleries–at which time the English mistrust of Impressionism and all its 'infections', burst forth once more with renewed fury and bitterness.

It is clear, then, that the closing decades of the nineteenth century saw dramatically changing attitudes to art, artists and their role in society. These changes were frequently labelled 'Impressionist', both by friends and foe. The artists concerned revealed a fundamentally altered understanding of the relationship between a picture, its author and its audience, and in this they owed much to Whistler and his French associates. Whether the paintings dealt abruptly with themes of modern life, or revealed a subtle and enigmatic response to the poetry of the visual world, these are absorbing works. They are distinguished by a preoccupation with the intrinsically beautiful qualities of paint, tone, handling and composition. Even more interesting, in some ways, is their articulation of contemporary concerns. Industrialization, urbanization, the threat of social change and technological onslaught, are all part of the debate. Excitement and uncertainty about the new cities and suburbs collide with one another. Attachment to land and sea relates nostalgia and gratitude, fear for loss and delight in possession. Perhaps above all, the message of these British Impressionist paintings is one of pride and even nationalism; it is not an uncertain and defensive insularity.

James McNeill Whistler
Nocturne in Black and Gold: The Firewheel
Oil on canvas, *Trustees of the Tate Gallery, London.*

James McNeill Whistler
A Shop with a Balcony
Oil on canvas, *Hunterian Art Gallery, University of Glasgow, Birnie Philip Bequest.*

Paul Maitland
Kensington Gardens
Oil on canvas, *Ashmolean Museum, Oxford.*

W. R. Sickert
The Red Shop – October Sun
Oil on wood, *Norfolk Museums Services, (Norwich Castle Musuem).*

Walter Richard Sickert
The Gallery of the Old Bedford
Oil on canvas, *Trustees of the National Museums and Galleries on Merseyside, Walker Art Gallery.*

Walter Richard Sickert
L'Hôtel Royal, Dieppe
Oil on wood, *Ferens Art Gallery, Hull City Museums and Art Galleries.*

Jacques Emile Blanche
Piccadilly Circus
Oil on canvas, *York City Art Gallery.*

Philip Wilson Steer
Figures on the Beach at Walberswick
Oil on canvas, *Trustees of the Tate Gallery, London.*

Philip Wilson Steer
Girls Running, Walberswick Pier
Oil on canvas, *Trustees of the Tate Gallery, London.*

William L. Wyllie
The Thames near Charing Cross
Oil on wood, *Nottingham Castle Museum.*

Stanhope Forbes
A Street in Brittany
Oil on canvas, *Trustees of the National Museums and Galleries on Merseyside, Walker Art Gallery.*

William Holt Yates Titcomb
Old Sea Dogs
Oil on canvas, *Nottingham Castle Museum.*

Henry Tuke
The Promise
Oil on canvas, *Trustees of the National Museums and Galleries on Merseyside, Walker Art Gallery.*

George Clausen
In the Orchard
Oil on canvas, *The City of Salford Museum and Art Gallery.*

Henry Herbert La Thangue
Tucking the Rick
Oil on canvas, *Mason, Owen & Partners.*

James Guthrie
Midsummer
Oil on canvas, *Royal Scottish Academy, Edinburgh.*

The Artists & their Paintings

Carte-de-visite, Whistler, 1865
Photograph courtesy of J. Maas

James McNeill Whistler

An American by birth, Whistler studied in Paris, before moving to London in 1859. His **At the Piano** was exhibited, and admired, at the R.A. in 1860. During the following years, however, his work became increasingly controversial.

Whistler's early artistic enthusiasm was for the Realist painter Courbet; but during the 1860s in London the persuasive appeal of the paintings and poetry of Dante Gabriel Rossetti, Swinburne and their circle, became more important. Excitement over the radical simplifications of Japanese prints and interest in the elusive poetry of Baudelaire and, later, of Mallarmé, began to prompt questions about the nature and purpose of art in society. By the 1870s, Whistler was developing an independence of vision which shocked many contemporaries.

In November 1878, following a virulent attack against his **Nocturne in Black and Gold: The Falling Rocket** which was shown at the Grosvenor Gallery, Whistler sued the critic, Ruskin, for libel. He won a farthing's damages but not his costs. Bankruptcy was the inevitable consequence. In the next year he left London for Venice, where he spent more than twelve months, producing numerous paintings, etchings and pastels, full of light and freshness, reflecting his renewed enthusiasm for working 'en plein air' and capturing effects of fleeting light and transient activity.

Whistler returned to London at the end of 1880 and, during the following decades, he established himself as a leading radical. He developed close friendships with some of the central figures of the Impressionist circle and soon became an enormously influential link between artists in Paris and London. Whistler worked in a variety of media; he also wrote, published and lectured. In all, he constantly emphasised that the artist could select any aspect of the natural world to paint; should not burden his theme with allegory or narrative, but attempt to convey something of his personal response; and, above all, should devote attention to the qualities of form and colour which provided the grammar and vocabulary of art.

In May 1884 and 1886 Whistler staged two major one-man exhibitions, 'Notes'-'Harmonies'-'Nocturnes', at Dowdeswell's. Included in these shows were numerous marvellous and evocative little panel paintings. These commanded considerable attention and helped to establish Whistler as the leading protagonist of radical art in Britain.

1.Nocturne in Black and Gold: The Firewheel
Oil on canvas, 21⅜ x 30 ins.

This picture was painted in the mid 1870s, at a time when Whistler was busy experimenting and creating images of extraordinary dynamism and variety of touch. The effects of the fireworks, brilliant against the night sky, are created with drips and spots of paint applied with astonishing freedom. It was the dramatic break from convention, represented by paintings such as this, which so outraged that most prominent of Whistler's critics, John Ruskin. When **Nocturne in Black and Gold: The Falling Rocket**–another painting of the firework entertainments at Cremorne Gardens–was exhibited at the opening show of the Grosvenor Gallery in 1877, Ruskin published his bitter attack which prompted Whistler to sue him for libel.

Lent by the Trustees of the Tate Gallery, London.

Cliffs and Breakers (detail)

Portrait Study of a Man (detail)

Winter Exhibition of the S.B.A.

2. Cliffs and Breakers

Oil on wood, 4⅞ x 8½ ins.

Possibly painted during the winter of 1883-4 when Whistler was working with Sickert on the coast near St. Ives. It has a delightful freshness and immediacy and provides an interesting comparison with Sickert's **Clodgy, Cornwall**, (No. 29) probably executed at the same time.

Lent by the Hunterian Art Gallery, University of Glasgow. Birnie Philip Bequest.

3. A Shop with a Balcony

Oil on wood, 8¾ x 5⅜ ins.

This casually intimate glimpse of a shop front is typical of work executed during the later 1880s and early 90s. The rich, gem-like colour of the figures, against the soft brown tones of the shop front, lends the whole a remarkably vivid intensity.

Lent by the Hunterian Art Gallery, University of Glasgow. Birnie Philip Bequest

4. Portrait Study of a Man

Oil on wood, 6⅝ x 4 ins.

Probably executed in the 1890s, this delightful little panel painting has a deftness of touch and a quiet intimacy which is so distinctive a feature of Whistler's portrait paintings of these years.

Lent by the Syndics of the Fitzwilliam Museum, Cambridge.

5. Winter Exhibition of the S.B.A.

Pen and ink on paper, 7⅞ x 6¼ ins.

This sketch of the winter 1886-7 exhibition of the S.B.A., staged just after Whistler had been elected President, reveals the careful hanging of the pictures and the suspended velarium of Indian muslin, introduced to create an even distribution of soft light.

Lent by the Visitors of the Ashmolean Museum, Oxford.

William Stott of Oldham

*T*he son of an Oldham mill owner, Stott attended the Manchester Academy of Fine Arts before travelling to Paris to study under Bonnat and Gérôme in 1879. He became a star pupil at the Ecole des Beaux Arts, and yet, even in work of the late 70s, it seems that he had learned from the Impressionists, as well as from his more officially admired teachers. He showed a painting entitled the **Wandering Musician** at the Liverpool Autumn Exhibition in 1878 and in a small, Corotesque picture of the same date, the deft touches of blue and red, against the generally brown tonality, suggest an awareness of a modified form of Impressionism.

During the early 80s, in France, Stott was known as a member of the 'Whistler Group'. This probably included Lavery and Alexander Roche, both to become leading members of the Glasgow School, and both also studying in Paris–at the Atelier Julian, rather than the Ecole. They spent several summers together at the artists' colony at Grès, together with R.A.M. Stevenson, Stott's great friend T. Millie Dow and–almost certainly–Stott himself.

Stott's painting **La Baignade**, awarded a gold medal at the Salon in 1882, might well have been painted in Grès. It was exhibited again at the Glasgow Institute in 1883, the year in which Bastien-Lepage's **Mendicant** was also on show. These two paintings brought a breath of French 'plein air' to those of the Glasgow group who had not themselves been to Paris.

Stott enjoyed early success at both the Salon and the Royal Academy. For most of the mid 1880s, however, he was absent from the Academy, demonstrating his loyalty to Whistler and the Royal Society of British Artists, of which he was elected a member in 1885. His **Portrait of My Friend, T.M.D.** (T. Millie Dow), was shown in 1886 and is a characteristic example of Stott's fascination for a Whistlerian style of portraiture, demonstrated again in his remarkable pastel study of his wife, probably executed in the late 1880s. These pictures have a simplicity and an intensity about them, in both composition and personality, which is captivating.

Whistler's influence is again quite clear in the extraordinary simplicity of the pastels executed in the mid 1880s. **Seascape** and **North Breeze** can be compared to the numerous little oil sketches of coastal scenes exhibited by Whistler in the 1884 Dowdeswell's exhibition, 'Notes'–'Harmonies'–'Nocturnes'. Indeed, like Whistler, Stott was accused of working to a formula; "a streak of blue above and a streak of green below".

When not in London or Paris, Stott spent his time in Cumberland. From here he sent more than one work entitled **Pastoral** to the R.S.B.A. **Pastoral: With Gorse**, which can probably be identified as **Ravenglass**, was on view in 1888. In these images of the landscape, and, indeed, in his portraits, it is possible to identify not only the impact of Whistler, but also the influence of Degas. The critic Alice Corkran had observed in 1889 that "Degas...this leader of the Impressionist School most influenced his style". There is even a suggestion that, while in Paris, Stott had received tuition from Lhermitte and Degas. Certainly, **A Summer Day**, a large, tightly organized composition of nude boys on the beach, which was exhibited at the R.S.B.A. in the winter of 1886-7, could be compared to early, large scale subject pictures by Degas.
(Alice Corkran, **Scottish Art Review**. April 1889. p. 320)

1888 was a turning point for Stott. A serious quarrel with Whistler resulted in a permanent rift. From this time on, Stott's paintings lost their wonderful simplicity, becoming larger, overwhelmingly elaborate and often allegorical. He continued to enjoy popularity, however, until 1900, when–as Whistler maliciously observed–"he died at sea, where he always was".

6. The North Breeze
Pastel on paper, 9 x 12 ins.
Lent by Oldham Art Gallery.

7. A Seascape
Pastel on paper, 9½ x 12½ ins.
Signed and dated 1884–which probably indicates a date for **The North Breeze** also–this is one of several small pastels, of exquisite simplicity, executed on the coast at about this time.
Lent by Oldham Art Gallery.

8. Woodland Scene, Brantrake
Pastel on paper, 9½ x 12½ ins.
This belongs to the mid 1880s, perhaps produced in c.1885, during a summer spent in Cumberland. Across a ground of soft grey and green, Stott has drawn a web of leaf and tree, in brilliant tones of rust, yellow, emerald and purple, conveying a sense of excitement and spontaneity.
Lent by Oldham Art Gallery.

9. The Artist's Wife
Pastel on paper, 22½ x 17 ins.
Stott obviously enjoyed working in pastel, using it with great breadth and freedom. The informality of the pose, the focus on

A Seascape (detail)

Woodland Scene, Brantrake

face and hands, the subtle handling of tones, and the careful placing of the figure on the paper, reveal a sophisticated understanding of the portraiture of both Whistler and Degas.
Lent by Manchester City Art Galleries.

10. Portrait of T. Millie Dow
Oil on canvas, 41 x 31⅞ ins.
This was probably exhibited as **Portrait of my Friend, T.M.D.** at the S.B.A. in 1886 (249). The figure of Millie Dow–who was also an artist–is presented at the forefront of the picture plane, conveying an immediacy and directness reminiscent of Degas, whom Stott certainly admired.
Lent by the National Gallery of Modern Art, Edinburgh.

11. A Summer Day
Oil on canvas, 50¾ x 73 ins.
This astonishing, large composition of nude boys, their features conveyed with photographic intensity and their figures almost etched against the flat expanse of sand, was shown at the 1886-7 winter exhibition of the S.B.A. (245). The critic, George Moore, objected to this picture, because "it is too large, it is a subject picture, it is traditional". Yet, although there are, indeed, a number of sketches which clearly indicate this to be a studio work, it is, nonetheless, a striking painting, clearly revealing the dramatic impact of Degas.
(George Moore, **Magazine of Art**, XII, 1888-9, p.296.)
Lent by Manchester City Art Galleries.

12. Ravenglass
Oil on canvas, 17¾ x 21 ins.
Probably **Pastoral: with Gorse**, shown at the R.S.B.A. in 1888 (122). The simplicity of the trees and sheep, together with the sharp intrusions of gorse, illustrate Stott's increasing interest in decoration, with strong, abstract impact. At the same time, the painting conveys the quality of light and atmosphere experienced on the west coast, between the sea and the Cumbrian Mountains.
Lent by Manchester City Art Galleries.

Paul Maitland, 1863-1909

An extraordinarily shy, retiring character, who suffered from physical disability, Paul Maitland was a close friend of Theodore Roussel, his confidante, protector and even his link to other artists. Maitland showed first at the R.S.B.A. in the winter of 1887-8 and then followed those other supporters of Whistler to the N.E.A.C. in 1888. He contributed six works to the 'London Impressionists'; but it seems that he showed less and less as he grew older.

Maitland's favourite haunts were Kensington Gardens and the Chelsea riverside. In paintings such as **Kensington Gardens**, there is a distinct reference to the low-toned, delicate landscapes of Corot. It is interesting to find that Corot's work had been exhibited in London since the 1860s and Whistler's friend, the dealer D.C. Thomson, published an admiring book on him in 1892. Yet, even though Maitland quite possibly never met Whistler, his seems to be the most potent influence. Indeed, the critic of the 'Art Journal' describing Maitland's work in 1907, noted "the veiled London of misty days, ..the uncrowded river, as he would not have seen it but for Whistler".
(**Paul Maitland at W.B.Paterson's Gallery**. 'Art Journal', 1907. p.282.)

It remains very difficult to identify the dates of Maitland's pictures. He almost always worked on a small scale, often on wooden panels of the kind favoured by Whistler, Sickert and their associates, when they were wandering about the city streets or painting in the wind and the spray by the sea. The wonderful little snow scene, **Cheyne Walk: the Corner of Beaufort Street** might be identified as **A Street in Winter** at the N.E.A.C. in 1888. **Barges, Chelsea Riverside, the 'Eighties** could be **Coal Barges**, shown at the N.E.A.C. in 1891. It is, however, all speculation. The large pastel **The Hollywood Arms, lit by a "Sugg" Gas-lamp**, (now at the Victoria and Albert Museum) was shown at the Glasgow Institute in the winter of 1890-91 and, again, at the N.E.A.C. a few months later. The critic D.S. MacColl referred to this as Maitland's single "bid for stronger realism". Yet even here the image is a rather mysterious, melancholy one. Almost invariably, his pictures convey something of the personality of the artist; self-effacing, silent, haunting.

13. Cheyne Walk, Sunshine
Oil on Canvas, 14 x 12 ins.
There is a breadth in the quality of the paint, an adventurousness in the composition here, which seems characteristic of some of the earlier paintings by Maitland. Possibly this can help to date this little picture to about 1887-8.
Lent by the York City Art Gallery.

14. Cheyne Walk, the Corner of Beaufort Street.
Oil on wood, 8¾ x 8½ ins.
Signed lower left, PM. Painted on a tiny, almost square panel, this might have been at the N.E.A.C. in 1888 as **A Street in Winter**, (48). Both this and **Cheyne Walk, Sunshine** reveal the impact of Roussel, Whistler and even, at a distance, of French Impressionism; there is a love of different lighting and seasonal effects, the intimate glimpse of everyday life, and carefully organised composition.
Lent by the Trustees of the Tate Gallery, London.

15. Barges, Chelsea Riverside, the 'Eighties
Oil on wood, 10⅜ x 12⅝ ins.
One of numerous small paintings which capture the busy movement of the barges on the river. Most seem to have been painted in about 1888-9.
Lent by the Trustees of the Tate Gallery, London.

16. Factories Bordering the River
Oil on canvas, 10⅛ x 14½ ins.
Lent by the Trustees of the Tate Gallery, London.

17. Boats on the Thames at Chelsea
Oil on canvas, 9 x 13 ins.
Lent by the National Museum of Wales, Cardiff.

18. A House seen through Trees and Shrubs
Oil on canvas, 16 x 12 ins.
The subtle command of tone is among the most distinctive of Maitland's characteristics. This lends his paintings a remarkable intensity.
Lent by the Visitors of the Ashmolean Museum, Oxford.

19. Kensington Gardens
Oil on canvas, 16 x 20 ins.
This is one of the larger, and possibly slighter later, of the many paintings of Kensington Gardens. The softly brushed, empty foreground, the line of trees cutting through the sunshine in the

Cheyne Walk, the Corner of Beaufort Steet (detail)

Factories Bordering the River (detail)

A House seen through Trees and Shrubs (detail)

middle distance, the few empty chairs delicately touched in—all convey a sense of isolation and even melancholy which seems to be more pronounced in the later work.

Lent by the Visitors of the Ashmolean Museum, Oxford.

20. Kensington Gardens, Vicinity of the Pond
Oil on canvas, 10 x 17⅞ ins.

Again, probably one of the later views of Kensington Gardens, possibly 1907. Maitland's touch seems to have become more delicate, his canvas somewhat larger, towards the end of his career. His colour remains extraordinarily subtle.

Lent by the Trustees of the Tate Gallery, London.

Theodore Roussel, 1847-1926

Roussel, a Frenchman driven out of the country by the Franco-Prussian war in 1872, settled in Chelsea, already a part of London inhabited by artists, including Whistler. The two seem to have met in about 1885. By the winter of 1886-7, Roussel was amongst those who showed at the R.S.B.A., demonstrating their support for their newly elected President.

Roussel's early interest in the painters of the Barbizon was important, for his pictures often display the dense paint and rather sombre tones characteristic of such French work. During the late 1880s, however, Roussel was often to be found in the company of Whistler, Sickert and Stott of Oldham, and in paintings exhibited from this time it is clear that his touch became more fluent, delicate and precise. **The Bathers** was shown at the R.S.B.A. in autumn 1887, in the same year as the impressive image of **The Reading Girl** (now at the Tate Gallery) appeared at the N.E.A.C. Both of these pictures are interesting in their preoccupation with the nude. It is clear that, during these years, a number of painters on both sides of the Channel explored ways in which the nude—that symbol of official success—could be presented in a naturalistic, rather than idealistic, manner. If **The Bathers** remains something of an idyll, **The Reading Girl** appears a much more confident and richly coloured vision of contemporary life, almost photographic in its stark contrasts of light and shade.

The human figure remained important to Roussel, lending much of his work the warmth and intimacy of daily life. The delicate picture of **The Artist's Wife**; the numerous coloured etchings to which he devoted much of his time; all have a tremendous immediacy. He also loved the Thames and the populous streets of Chelsea; his contribution of seven pictures to the 'London Impressionists' exhibition were almost all scenes of this kind. Even pictures such as the exquisite little **Grey and Silver: Flowers in a Vase**, convey a sense of devoted attachment to the poetry of the everyday world.

Roussel's poetry, however, was combined with what was probably an even greater preoccupation with scientific experiment and discovery. He seems to have been investigating the optical impact of different colours at about the time he met Whistler and this remained a passionate concern throughout his life. From his awareness of the distinction between the colour of pigment and of light, it must be assumed that Roussel had studied the colour theories of Chevreul, first published in 1839, available in an English translation in 1854, and reissued during the 1880s. It is fascinating to compare such an analytical approach to the relationship between colour and light, with those parallel investigations being undertaken in France.

40

Another of the group of 'Whistler followers', Mortimer Menpes, observed at this time that they all "became prismatic" and "began to paint in spots and dots...stripes and bands". It is quite probable that it was Roussel's dedication to such concerns which offered an example to his colleagues.

21. The Bathers
Oil on canvas, 15½ x 11½ ins.
Shown at the R.S.B.A. winter exhibition of 1887-8 (207). It makes an interesting comparison with William Stott's **A Summer Day**, shown a year earlier.
Private Collection.

22. Portrait of the Artist's Wife
Oil on canvas, 72 x 39 ins.
Private Collection.

23. Grey and Silver. Flowers in a Vase
Oil on canvas, 24 x 20¼ ins.
Lent by the Art Gallery and Museum, Royal Pavilion, Brighton.

24. Battersea from Cheyne Walk
Oil on panel, 12 x 16 ins.
Almost certainly executed in the late 1880s, when Roussel and Maitland were often to be found working near the Thames, imbuing these familiar sights with a quiet, personal poetry.
Private Collection.

25. Approaching Storm, Dover
Oil on canvas, 23 x 19½ ins.
This painting reveals that preoccupation with effects of light and weather, particularly at the coast, which characterised so much of the painting of the Whistler circle during these years
Lent by the Lincolnshire County Council, Recreational Services, Usher Gallery, Lincoln.

26. Pierrot en Pied, Portrait of Lady AC
Etching.
During his career, Roussel became increasingly absorbed in graphic media. Like Whistler, he etched on the spot and devoted endless attention to the printing of the images. This little picture presents Lady Archibald Campbell dressed as a pierrot for a "pastoral play" which was staged in August, 1888. The event was attended not only by Roussel, but also by Whistler–a great admirer of Lady Archie–and by Oscar Wilde.
(**The Hawk**, 14.8.88.)
Lent by the Victoria and Albert Museum, London.

27. Chelsea Palaces, Chelsea Embankment.
Etching.
Chelsea and Kensington provided much material for Roussel's graphic works. These tiny images reveal a fascination for casual glimpses of everyday life, for concise definition of architecture, and the pattern of light and shade over surfaces. Roussel's biographer, Frank Rutter, quoted Roussel as insisting that, "anything I have done in etching I owe absolutely to the influence of Whistler". By 1899, however, Roussel's etchings were becoming even more ambitious, and he exhibited some colour prints at the Goupil Gallery in London in July 1899.
Lent by the Victoria and Albert Museum, London.

Walter Richard Sickert, 1860-1942
Sickert first met Whistler in 1879, describing him as the "only painter left alive who has immense genius". By 1882, Sickert

had left the Slade to become Whistler's assistant.

During the winter of 1883-4, Sickert and Whistler, together with Mortimer Menpes, spent some weeks in Cornwall. They were painting 'en plein air', using small, wooden panels. In the summer of 1885 Sickert showed four works at the S.B.A., including three seascapes, **Paragon and Westcliff, Ramsgate**, (which might be identified as **View of Ramsgate**), **Barnoon Field, St. Ives, Cornwall** and **Clodgy, Cornwall**. The latter is very Whistlerian, both in size and execution and can be closely compared with Whistler's own **Cliffs and Breakers**.

The same could be said of another seascape, **Dieppe La Plage**, perhaps **The Breakwater**, shown at the S.B.A. in the winter of 1885-6. Again, it is deft, vigorous, precise in touch. It is clear that Sickert was enthusiastic in his attempts to capture some expression of a fleeting moment of time in paintings such as these. Like Whistler, he worked not only at the sea, but also enjoyed the little shops and street corners of the city. **The Red Shop**, from the mid 1880s, and **L'Hôtel Royal**, c. 1900, are witness to the desire Sickert expressed, in his preface for the 1889 'London Impressionists' exhibition, to "render the magic and the poetry" of daily life.

Many of these paintings were executed in Dieppe where, from the mid 80s, Sickert spent many summer months in the company of Whistler, Jacques-Emile Blanche and Degas. It is well known that when, in 1883, Sickert accompanied Whistler's **Portrait of the Artist's Mother** to the Paris Salon, he had been equipped with letters of introduction to both Degas and Manet. The latter had been too ill to receive him, but the contact with Degas was to be a very important one. While Sickert had first shown at the R.S.B.A. as a 'pupil of Whistler', when he quit that body for the N.E.A.C. in 1888, there was no longer any sign of apprenticeship. Sickert's individuality as a painter was, instead, asserted with numerous images of public entertainment, particularly of the music halls. The majority of his six paintings in the 'London Impressionists' were of such scenes, as were many of the works he sent to the N.E.A.C. until the turn of the century. The glowing picture of **Minnie Cunningham at the Old Bedford** appeared in the winter of 1892; **The Sisters Lloyd** in the summer of 1894; **The Gallery of the Old Bedford** appeared in winter 1895 as **The Boy I love is up in the Gallery**. Even as late as 1906 Sickert was still pursuing these themes and he showed one of several marvellously evocative sketches of the music hall audience, **Noctes Ambrosianae**, in the summer of 1906. Modern life, in many of its urban guises, remained fascinating to Sickert; a fascination that owed much to Degas.

Both Whistler and Degas were to remain important to Sickert throughout his life, despite his express reaction against Whistler, published in 'Art News' in 1910. If, in later years, Sickert felt that his mentor's approach had been too precious, he also recognised that, above all, the barriers of British insularity had been broached;

If Whistler has himself left, in an interesting and passionately felt lifework, a contribution to our better understanding of the tradition of painting, he has also done another thing. He has sent the more intelligent of the generation that succeeds him to the springs whence he drew his own art—to French soil. (W.R. Sickert, **The New Life of Whistler**, 'Fortnightly Review', December 1908).

28. Violets
Oil on wood, 4½ x 8 ins.
Lent by the Victoria Art Gallery, Bath.

29. Clodgy Point, Cornwall

Oil on wood, 4⅞ x 8½ ins.

Probably **Clodgy, Cornwall**, shown at the S.B.A. in 1885 (228). This evocative little picture can be directly compared with Whistler's **Cliffs and Breakers**, (No. 2) painted when Whistler, Sickert and Mortimer Menpes were working together at St. Ives, Cornwall, in January 1884. The size of the wooden panels are almost identical–another reflection of their closeness at this time.

Lent by the Hunterian Art Gallery, University of Glasgow.

30. Dieppe, La Plage

Oil on wood, 8¾ x 13¾ ins.

Wendy Baron suggests that this might be **The Breakwater**, exhibited at the S.B.A. by Sickert as 'a pupil of Whistler', in the winter of 1885-6 (223)
(Wendy Baron, **Sickert.** Phaidon 1973 p.299)

Lent by Manchester City Art Galleries.

31. Sea Piece

Oil on wood, 9¾ x 5¾ ins.

Lent by the Scottish National Gallery of Modern Art, Edinburgh.

Sea Piece

32. A Shop in Dieppe

Oil on canvas, 13¾ x 10½ ins.

For years Dieppe remained one of Sickert's favourite haunts. He spent his summers there regularly and lived there from 1898, after his divorce. From the style of the signature and the character of touch and tone, this picture would appear to date from the 1890s. It is interesting to compare this with Whistler's **A Shop with a Balcony** (No. 3).

Lent by the Hunterian Art Gallery, University of Glasgow.

33. The Red Shop, October Sun

Oil on wood, 10½ x 14 ins.

Painted on a panel of a size almost identical to **A Shop in Dieppe**, this again reveals Sickert's growing confidence in working with a range of subtle tones and responding to effects of light and atmosphere.

Lent by Norfolk Museums Service (Castle Museum, Norwich).

34. View of Ramsgate

Oil on canvas, 25 x 29½ ins.

Lent by the Kirklees Metropolitan Council, Huddersfield Art Gallery.

35. L'Hôtel Royal

Oil on canvas, 18¼ x 21¾ ins.

Lent by the Ferens Art Gallery, Hull City Museums and Art Galleries.

36. St. Mark's Facade, Venice

Oil on paper and panel, 8¾ x 11¾ ins.

Venice was another centre frequented by Sickert. He first spent some time in the city in the summer of 1895, his last visit was in 1903-4. By this time, Sickert had moved away from the practice of producing his paintings 'en plein air'. Instead, he preferred to work in the studio, from colour notes, photographs and quick sketches. This little panel has a freshness about it which suggests it might have been among the "Drawings in plenty (which) were done on the spot".
(Alfred Thornton, **W.R.Sickert,**'Artwork', Vol. VI, no. 21, Spring 1930, p.15.)

Lent by the Visitors to the Ashmolean Museum, Oxford.

St. Mark's Facade, Venice

43

The Theatre of the Young Artists (detail)

Noctes Ambrosianae (detail)

37. The Theatre of the Young Artists
Oil on hardboard, 20½ x 25½ ins.

One of the numerous images of the theatre, this particular painting was first purchased by Mr W.H. Stephenson of Southport in the 1920s. He reported that "Sickert was greatly pleased on hearing this news, for he imagined that he had been forgotten..."
(Marjorie Lilley, **Sickert. The Painter and his Circle.** Noyes Press 1973. p.156.)
Lent by the Atkinson Gallery, Sefton Metropolitan Borough Libraries and Art Services.

38. Minnie Cunningham at the Old Bedford
Oil on canvas, 30⅛ x 25⅛ ins.

This wonderfully luminous painting was almost certainly shown at the N.E.A.C. in the winter of 1892 (91).
Lent by the Trustees of the Tate Gallery, London.

39. George Moore
Oil on canvas, 23¾ x 19¾ ins.

This was shown at the N.E.A.C. in the winter of 1891 (48). George Moore, the art critic of the **Speaker** from 1891 to 1895, was a vocal supporter of many exhibitors at the N.E.A.C. He, like so many of his artist colleagues, had studied in Paris in 1872, where he attended the Ecole des Beaux Arts and the Académie Julian. He came to know the French Impressionists, including Manet and Degas, both of whom also painted his portrait. Moore produced several accounts of his experiences in France, among the most interesting of which was **Modern Painters**, published in 1893.
Lent by the Trustees of the Tate Gallery, London.

40. The Gallery of the Old Bedford
Oil on canvas, 30 x 23½ ins.

Exhibited at the N.E.A.C. in winter 1895 as **The Boy I love is up in the Gallery** (73).
Lent by the Trustees of the National Museums and Galleries on Merseyside, Walker Art Gallery, Liverpool.

41. Noctes Ambrosianae
Oil on canvas, 25 x 30 ins.

This striking picture, with its sombre but subtle colouring, was shown at the N.E.A.C. in the summer of 1906 (123). It is characteristic of Sickert's later paintings of the theatre and music hall, concentrating attention on the audience and architecture, rather than on the stage.
Lent by Nottingham Castle Museum.

Jacques-Emile Blanche, 1861-1942

Parisian-born Jacques-Emile Blanche was a frequent visitor to Dieppe, where he was host to many visiting artists, both French and English. In his Book, **Portraits of a Lifetime**, published in 1937, Blanche recalls his friendships with Whistler, Sickert and George Moore, as well as Degas and the painter of stylish society portraits, Paul Helleu. There is no doubt that Blanche's engaging personality, and his elegant, painterly technique, secured him many friends, who benefited from his cosmopolitan attitudes.

42. Piccadilly Circus
Oil on canvas, 27½ x 37 ins.
Lent by York City Art Gallery.

Philip Wilson Steer, 1860-1942

Steer, like a number of his colleagues, exhibited at the R.S.B.A. from 1885-1888, and at the N.E.A.C. from its inception in 1886. **Surf**, a vigorously executed sea study, at the British Artists in the winter of 1887-8, already indicates some familiarity with the idea of painting 'en plein air' and is an early example of Steer's continuing fascination for the coast and countryside.

Steer first went to Paris to study in 1882, where he found himself amongst that group of English and American students which included John Lavery and William Stott of Oldham. From the fact that he left France in 1884–like several of his English-speaking colleagues–because of his failure to pass an examination in the French language, it is clear that he remained, to some extent at least, isolated from his French colleagues. Nevertheless, it is probable that he saw some paintings by the Impressionists, and visited the large posthumous Manet show held in January 1884. Certainly, Steer's early work reveals an astonishing array of personal and experimental reactions to some of the radical developments of his time.

Knucklebones, (now at the Ipswich Art Gallery) was included in the 'London Impressionists' in 1889. It has a dense, tapestry-like surface and it comes as no surprise to discover that the techniques of Neo-Impressionism were attracting considerable attention in London at this time. Also at the 'London Impressionists' was **The Beach, Walberswick**. There are two paintings of this subject now in the Tate, both probably from this date: **The Beach at Walberswick** and **Figures on the Beach, Walberswick**. Again, there are touches in the sea and sand of complementary colours, applied with soft, dotting brush over a broadly painted base. It is interesting that the critic D.S. MacColl, who did not like such paintings, recognised the impact of Neo-Impressionism; and when Lucien Pissarro met Steer, at a Symposium on Impressionism, organised by the Art Workers' Guild in May 1891, he wrote to his father that Steer "divides his tones as we do, and is very intelligent". (ed. John Rewald, **Camille Pissarro–Letters to Lucien**, London 1943).

The central figure in French Neo-Impressionism was, of course, Georges Seurat. His extraordinary image, **La Grande Jatte**, was shown with the Belgian group, 'Les XX', in 1887. In 1889 and 1891 Steer and Seurat were both invited to exhibit with the group. There can be no doubt that not only the analysis of colour, but also the enigmatic poetry of Seurat's paintings, fascinated Steer. Intense and haunting are the pictures of the beach at Walberswick; those already discussed and the **Girls Running: Walberswick Pier**, with its heightened colour and densely encrusted paint.

It was at this time that Steer conceived an admiration for Rose Pettigrew, a young model who worked for Whistler as well as for Steer. Rose and her sister Lily, as well as other young girls, became the subjects of numerous studies, all of which are imbued with the intensity of fleeting passion. Several of these, such as the **Girl in a Blue Dress**, are executed on small, wooden panels of the kind used by Whistler, Sickert and their associates. In their precision, delicacy and gem-like scale, they reflect an exquisite melancholy that seems to have a universal as well as personal significance.

43. Surf

Oil on canvas, 6¼ x 29⅛ ins.

The sea provided a source of constant fascination for Steer. He frequently painted along the French coast, as well as at favoured

Surf (detail)

English spots, such as Walberswick in Suffolk. This is one of the earliest images of the sea and its most distinctive feature is the long, horizontal format, possibly influenced by Whistler and Sickert. Yet Steer's touch is more heavy and vigorous, suggesting a familiarity with the work of Courbet or even Manet.

Steer exhibited only four paintings at the R.S.B.A. and this was shown in the winter of 1887-8 (364).
Lent by the Syndics of the Fitzwilliam Museum, Cambridge.

44. Figures on the Beach at Walberswick
Oil on canvas, 24 x 24 ins.
Numerous studies of Walberswick appear in sketchbooks from about 1888-9. These were years in which Steer was experimenting, not only with his colour and technique, but also with mood. The intense personality of paintings such as this were noted by contemporaries, including the critic D.S.MacColl, who was somewhat disconcerted by what he viewed as theatricality.
Lent by the Trustees of the Tate Gallery, London.

The Beach at Walberswick (detail)

45. The Beach at Walberswick
Oil on canvas, 23¾ x 30 ins.
This painting is signed and dated 1891, but it is very heavily worked and numerous studies of this curve of shingle can be found in sketch books not later than 1889. The charmingly precise details–the shoes, the little dogs, the figures on the distant shingle, the brilliant tendrils of hair–tend to emphasise the broad, almost unworldly simplicity of the composition. The fascination for bright red hair is strongly Pre-Raphaelite in flavour, reflecting a growing taste for enigmatic, slightly decadent qualities, found on both sides of the Channel.
Possibly this picture was included in the 1889 London Impressionist exhibition, as **The Beach, Walberswick** (33).
Lent by the Trustees of the Tate Gallery, London.

46. Girls Running, Walberswick Pier
Oil on canvas, 24¾ x 36½ ins.
Again, a very heavily worked painting, the encrusted surface probably representing successive experiments from about 1889, until it was exhibited at Steer's first one-man show at the Goupil Gallery in 1894. The bold colours, and the twin figures, poised forever as they run, create an intensely poetic, even a melancholy, image. It must have been with paintings such as this in mind that, in 1891, at a Symposium on 'Impressionism' at the Art Workers' Guild, Steer delivered a paper. Here he declared that, "Impressionism bears the same relation to painting that poetry does to journalism".
Lent by the Trustees of the Tate Gallery, London.

Girl in a Blue Dress (detail)

47. Two Girls on Walberswick Beach
Oil on wood, 9⅞ x 13⅞ ins.
Lent by the Plymouth Museum and Art Gallery.

48. Girl in a Blue Dress
Oil on wood, 10¾ x 8¼ ins.
At the 'London Impressionists' Steer showed a portrait of **Pretty Rosie Pettigrew** (35), which seems to mark the beginning of his preoccupation with this young model. In a brief autobiography, originally written for D.S.MacColl, Rosie Pettigrew relates how she often posed for Whistler's "charming little pastels" in the late 1880s, while at the same time modelling for Steer for one day in the week. This tiny, poetic painting of Rosie in a blue dress can be dated to the early 90s, partly because

of the use of a wood panel, and also because a related painting, **The Blue Dress** was exhibited at the N.E.A.C. in 1892 (60), accompanied by a lengthy Latin title: "Molle meum levibus cor est violabile telis/Et semper causa est cur ego semper amem" (My soft heart is always liable to injury by light weapons/And the perpetual reason is that I am always in love).
(Bruce Laughton, **Philip Wilson Steer**, Oxford University Press, 1971. See Appendix, p.113).
Lent by the Trustees of the Tate Gallery, London.

49. The Sprigged Frock
Pastel, 23½ x 23½ ins.
Lent by the William Morris Gallery, (and Brangwyn Gift), London Borough of Waltham Forest.

The Sprigged Frock

50. Young Girl in a White Dress
Oil on canvas, 19⅝ x 16⅝ ins.
Signed and dated 1892, this is one of several paintings of young girls. There is certainly a reminiscence of portraits by Whistler, most obviously of the 1873 **Harmony in Grey and Green, Miss Cecily Alexander**, now in the Tate Gallery, London. But there is an added element, a disturbing petulance, even a melancholy. These images have a strong sensual dimension; they also seem to convey an intensely personal representation of the fleeting nature of time and experience.
Lent by Manchester City Art Galleries.

51. Schoolgirl Standing by a Door
Oil on canvas, 30¼ x 25 ins.
Once again, an evocative little image of a young girl conveys something of the peculiar and moving intensity of Steer's art during these years.
Lent by the Metropolitan Borough of Wirral, Williamson Art Gallery, Birkenhead.

Schoolgirl Standing by a Door (detail)

Sidney Starr, 1857-1925

The Art Workers' Guild Symposium on Impressionism, organised in 1891, received papers on the subject not only from Steer and Sickert, but also from Sidney Starr, included in those described as "the shining lights of the N.E.A.C." by Herbert Horne when writing to Lucien Pissarro in that year. (Letter dated 20.4.91. Pissarro papers, Ashmolean Museum, Oxford.).

Starr had come to London from Hull in 1874, having won a Slade scholarship. He soon encountered Whistler, whom he greatly admired, and his contributions to the R.S.B.A. reveal a dramatic change in subject matter, from appealing genre themes, to simple images of the countryside, portraits and the daily life of the city. Starr was much in Whistler's company in the late 1880s and, like his colleagues, he evidently used a box of panels, easily carried about with him, and always available to capture a fleeting image in paint. The **Fête Day** is one such panel, which must date from the mid 1880s; a marvellously swift, evocative work.

From little panels such as this it is clear that Starr had the ability to explore a tremendously subtle range of tone. This is evident again in his stylish, Whistlerian portraits; **Miss Gertrude Kingston** at the R.S.B.A. in 1888, and the **Study in Blue and Grey** shown at the N.E.A.C. in the winter of 1891.

Starr was included at the 'London Impressionists' exhibition in 1889. He showed a variety of works, displaying considerable versatility, both in scale and in subject matter. Perhaps one of the most interesting images was **The City Atlas**, (now in the National Gallery of Canada, Ottawa). A view of London streets

Miss Gertrude Kingston (detail)

Study in Blue and Grey (detail)

from the top of an omnibus, it reflects the contemporary fascination for scenes of modern, urban life; a fascination inspired not only by Whistler, but also by Degas, who first exhibited at the N.E.A.C. in 1888.

52. Miss Gertrude Kingston
Oil on canvas, 42⅝ x 32⅝ ins.

This striking image of the actress, in her riding habit, was the last painting shown by Starr at the R.S.B.A., in 1888 (140). It has a sharpness of form and a richness of colour which commands attention, revealing the artist's skill as a portrait painter.
Lent by the Ferens Art Gallery, Hull City Museums and Art Galleries.

53. Study in Blue and Grey
Oil on canvas, 75 x 42¼ins.

Shown at the 1891 winter exhibition of the N.E.A.C., (44), this was lent by that familiar patron–herself a painter–Mrs Cyprian Williams. Again, the simplicity of composition and subtle handling of colour, reveal something of Whistler and Degas, both of whom were greatly admired by Starr.
Lent by the Trustees of the Tate Gallery, London.

54. Fête Day
Oil on wood, 5½ x 9¾ ins.

In this little picture, which must date from the mid 1880s, Starr reveals a very subtle command of tone, with a wide variety of green, rust, pink, red and slate, unified by the warm red hue of the panel on which it is painted.
Lent by York City Art Gallery.

William L. Wyllie, 1851-1931

Wyllie was trained at the Royal Academy Schools, and achieved considerable success in his career, with marine paintings and etchings, often depicting Britain's naval power.

The artist exhibited at the R.A. and at the Society of British Artists, where he first showed as early as 1875. Many of the paintings–both oils and watercolours–indicate his preoccupation with images of the sea and river and also reflect fairly frequent visits to France and the Low Countries. He was obviously not, however, an enthusiastic follower of Whistler and his associates, for he showed no more at the S.B.A., after 1886, when Whistler was elected President.

Nevertheless, Wyllie must have become involved with some of the more radical artistic ideas during the late 1880s, and from 1889-1893 he submitted work to the N.E.A.C. During these years he seems to have experimented with his technique and composition, often employing tiny scale, or strong, vertical format, to enhance the dramatic impact of his paintings. He was also absorbed by effects of changing light and atmosphere.

55. The Thames near Charing Cross
Oil on wood, 6¾ x 10 ins.

In this river scene, painted in 1892, the tiny figures push their barge through the sparkling water. Behind them loom the dark silhouettes of public buildings, bulky railway sheds, factories, smoking chimneys and spires–all the clutter of urban life. The contrast between the timeless poetry of the river and the busy reality of industrial London is epitomised in the two river craft

at the far bank: one a sailing barge, one a tug with a smoking funnel.
Lent by Nottingham Castle Museum.

56. Romney Marsh
Oil on canvas, 8 x 16¼ ins.
Wyllie lived in Rochester, Kent, in the 1890s, and was fascinated by the vast landscapes of flat, marshy lands around the coast. Characteristic is the contrast between the timeless expanses of nature and the impact of industrialisation, represented by the smoke stacks of distant vessels beyond the horizon.
Lent by Nottingham Castle Museum.

Francis Bate

Francis Bate was active within the N.E.A.C., being elected to the committee, of which he became secretary, in 1888. His contributions to the shows reveal his interest in effects of light and in the changing seasons of the year.

Bate was closely associated with the circle of friends which surrounded Sickert in the late 1880s, and he was amongst the group showing as 'London Impressionists' in 1889, when he presented five works.

57. The Weeping Ash
Oil on canvas, 24 x 20 ins.
Bate showed regularly at the N.E.A.C., until 1906. Paintings entitled **The Weeping Ash** were exhibited in the winter of 1895 (74), and again in the summer of 1905 (62). It seems quite possible that these two were, in fact, the same painting, for by the early 1900s Bate was more active as a portraitist than a painter of landscape. Certainly, this picture reveals much of the quiet, perceptive approach to a simple image which was typical of Bate's work.
Lent by Reading Art Gallery.

Arthur Studd, 1863-1919

Arthur Studd was amongst Whistler's last close friends. He lived nearby and frequently visited Whistler at 74 Cheyne Walk, in 1902, during the final months of his life. Had it not been for Studd's bequest to the National Gallery of three major paintings, Whistler would have been even more badly represented than he is in England. It is to Studd that we owe the presence in the Tate Gallery of **The Little White Girl: Symphony in White, No.2, Nocturne in Blue and Silver: Cremorne Lights** and the **Nocturne in Black and Gold: The Firewheel**.

Studd had been a pupil at the Slade, under Legros, from 1888-9. He had followed this with a spell in Paris at the Académie Julian, and had from there travelled to Le Pouldu, in Brittany, in 1890. Here it seems certain that Studd met Gauguin and Meyer de Haan, also in search of a rural retreat. Although there are no direct references to such a meeting, Studd's great friend, Alfred Thornton, noted that Gauguin and his colleague had already moved to the greater seclusion of the inn of Mlle. Henry by the time he himself joined Studd in Brittany. To the second exhibition of the International Society, held in 1899, Studd sent **Beside a River in Brittany**. (A. Thornton, **The Diary of an Art Student of the 90s** London, 1938, p.8).

Romney Marsh (detail)

The Weeping Ash

Studd seems to have joined the circle of Whistler's close friends in about 1894. In a letter of that year he refers to "the great artistic debt that I am proud to acknowledge". Something of this debt is manifest in the small panel painting, **Washing Day**, one of several such casually intimate images of domesticity executed by Studd in the mid 1890s.

Of all the letters written by Studd to Whistler, the most fascinating must be one written from Papeete, Tahiti, in 1897. Here, Studd exhorts his 'chèr maître' to join him; "we have had beautiful cloudy weather ever since my arrival a month ago and the day would be for you full of sea pieces and the night full of nocturnes". Studd even exhibited a South Seas subject at the N.E.A.C. in the winter of 1898, **Fa Inpenga**. (Glasgow University, Whistler letters, GU BP II S/52. 22.6.97)

Studd's final submission to the N.E.A.C. was in 1901, but he continued to exhibit in London in the following years, particularly at the Goupil Gallery. He showed a number of Venetian paintings in 1907-8, having travelled extensively after Whistler's death. It is possible that he also visited Venice in the late 90s; certainly, the delicious little **Venetian Twilight**, so delicately Whistlerian in touch, is painted on a panel of exactly the same dimensions as other, more domestic paintings of this date.

58. Washing Day

Oil on wood, 8½ x 6¼ ins.

Once again, the artist is working on a small wooden panel or 'pochade', to enable him to note with ease the intimate glimpses of the world around him. The colour here is rich and brilliant; in its firm application and rather dry quality there are resonances of Gauguin. The picture probably dates from the mid 1890s, shortly after Studd had first met Whistler, whose influence is also discernible in this marvellous painting.

Lent by York City Art Gallery.

59. Venetian Twilight

Oil on wood, 5 x 8½ ins.

Studd seems to have travelled extensively from about 1903 to 1908, undoubtedly spending some of this time in Venice. He exhibited several paintings and etchings of the city, many executed on tiny, wooden panels and displaying an exquisite sense of tonal control.

Lent by York City Art Gallery.

60. A Venetian Lyric

Oil on wood, 9½ x 15¾ ins.

This is just one of several paintings by this name, probably produced in about 1907. The title indicates the very deliberate preoccupation with poetic or musical terminology, demanding an empathetic response to an intense, personal vision.

Lent by the Trustees of the Tate Gallery, London.

Stanhope Forbes

*I*f Stanhope Forbes was not the first artist to settle in Newlyn, he was one of the first to draw public attention to the work of the School, especially after the success of his **A Fish Sale on a Cornish Beach** at the Royal Academy in 1885.

Having been a student at the Royal Academy Schools, Forbes' first trip to Paris was in 1880, where he attended the studio of Bonnat. Like so many of his compatriots, Forbes worked in the French countryside during the summers, travelling to Brittany in 1881 with his friend La Thangue. The enchanting **A Street in Brittany** was painted at Cancale in this year and shown at the Royal Academy in 1882, the same year in which La Thangue exhibited **The Boat-building Yard** at the Grosvenor Gallery. Both works reveal a deep admiration for the 'square brush' technique and the rural imagery of Bastien-Lepage; on the latter's death in 1884, Forbes lamented "the greatest artist of our age".

One of the most distinctive features of Newlyn work is the manifest dedication to working 'en plein air'; certainly Stanhope Forbes revelled in the struggles occasioned by his determination to paint outside, no matter what difficulties were presented. The scale of these paintings is often quite large–not for them the habitual use of small panels on which to capture exquisite glimpses of a fleeting world. Indeed, Forbes obviously distrusted Whistler and his "gang", and strongly disapproved of his future wife's admiration for the 'master'. He expressed himself "astonished to find the impressionists in great force" at the N.E.A.C. of 1888, describing Sickert's picture–**Gatti's Hungerford Palace of Varieties: Second Turn of Miss Katie Lawrence**–as vulgar and tawdry. And, it is clear, the antagonism was mutual, for it can only have been Stanhope Forbes and his colleagues whom Sickert had in mind when he wrote to J.E. Blanche in 1889 of "the dull but powerful section of the N.E.A.C....whose touch is square and who all paint alike".

Together with one or two other Newlyners, Forbes had attended the inaugural meetings of the N.E.A.C.; in fact, his association with the group was doubtlessly viewed as a considerable asset by the financial backer, W.J. Laidlay, after Forbes' success at the Royal Academy only the year before. Forbes ceased exhibiting at the New English in 1889, however, and by 1892 was elected an Associate of the R.A.

61. A Street in Brittany

Oil on canvas, 41 x 29⅞ ins.

Signed and dated "à Cancale 1881", this painting obviously preoccupied Forbes for several months, between July and October, 1881. In writing of his work to his mother, Forbes makes clear his fascination with the variety of working figures, in their picturesque clothes. The aged, rugged character of the setting obviously also appealed. Here was an image of an old, simple society–although Forbes' letters reveal his consciousness that it was also a harsh society.

He remarked, almost with relief, that he was working on a figure in the shade, which extended the amount of time he could devote to the picture. It is interesting to note this preoccupation with the effects of weather and light, despite the fact that the painting clearly reveals, in the discrepancies of scale, that it was worked on over a considerable period.

(See letters of Stanhope Forbes to his mother, in the collection of the artist's family. Quoted by Fox and Greenacre, **Artists of the Newlyn School**, Newlyn Orion Galleries, 1979. p.73.)

Lent by the Trustees of the National Museums and Galleries on Merseyside, Walker Art Gallery, Liverpool.

62. Evening, Workers Return

Oil on canvas, 23½ x 19¾ ins.

By 1884, Forbes had rediscovered Newlyn. The place and its working people were to provide the majority of his subjects for the rest of his career, even after he was elected a Royal Academician in 1910.

Lent by the Gray Museum and Art Gallery, Hartlepool Borough Council.

63. Gala Day at Newlyn
Oil on canvas, 41¾ x 53¾ ins.
Lent by the Gray Museum and Art Gallery, Hartlepool Borough Council.

Thomas Cooper Gotch, 1854-1931

*F*or Gotch, training in London—at Heatherly's and the Slade—was followed by a spell in Paris in 1880. Here, he worked with several of his former Slade companions, including H.S. Tuke and Caroline Yates, who was to become his wife in 1881.

Back in London, Gotch was very active in the establishment of the N.E.A.C. and worked closely with W.J. Laidlay who boldly provided financial backing for the venture in its early stages.

The Silver Hour (detail)

In 1883 Gotch and his wife settled in Newlyn, where they continued to work for much of their life. They became friendly with Stanhope and Elizabeth Forbes and other members of the Newlyn School and Gotch's **Sharing Fish**, which was exhibited at the Royal Academy in 1891, reveals the characteristic Newlyn devotion to scenes of rustic realism. Many of his paintings, however, are much daintier in style and execution, more fluently painted and subtly toned. **The Silver Hour** and **The Estuary, Etaples** are almost Whistlerian in touch, with a pensive, almost melancholy quality.

64. The Estuary, Etaples
Oil on wood, 8 x 10 ins.
Lent by Alfred East Gallery, Kettering Borough Council

65. The Silver Hour
Oil on canvas, 13½ x 21 ins.
Lent by Alfred East Gallery, Kettering Borough Council

William Holt Yates Titcomb, 1858-1930

*T*itcomb, like so many of the artists in this exhibition, studied in England and then moved on to France. There he was influenced by what he saw of the Impressionists, but especially interested in the work of Bastien-Lepage. On his return to England, Titcomb joined his compatriots working in Newlyn, but he was not a permanent resident. He exhibited at the Royal Academy, and also at other venues. He appeared at the R.S.B.A., as an elected member, from 1891 until 1894. It is interesting to observe that he showed works of a rather literary character, or small sketches and domestic portraits, often in pastel. To the N.E.A.C., where he showed from 1889 to 1897, he submitted works of a different type; images of working folk in Cornwall, or, in 1897, impressions of Venice.

66. Old Sea Dogs
Oil on canvas, 62 x 48 ins.
This rather splendid painting, with its fresh and decorative paintwork and sparking light, was exhibited at the R.A. in 1891. The figures of the old fishermen are almost heroic in character, lending the whole a faintly sentimental appeal.
Lent by Nottingham Castle Museum.

Henry Scott Tuke, 1858-1929

*T*uke was a student at the Slade in the 1870s, a close friend of Gotch, with whom he often went sketching. He followed this with travels in France, which he first visited as early as 1877, even attending the studio of Bastien-Lepage in February 1882. Here he saw "many things of surpassing beauty".

In France, the cosmopolitan Jacques- Emile Blanche was a friend; indeed, in 1883 Tuke was painting in a studio in Blanche's house. The Paris Salon of 1882 saw the success of William Stott, whose **La Baignade** was awarded a gold medal. His evocative **Le Passeur** was also on show, and particularly attracted the attention of Tuke.

Tuke was a keen traveller, studying in Belgium and Italy in the 1880s and, in the early 1890s, spending time on the Mediterranean coast. His interest in the silver tonality and square brush of the Naturalists was gradually modified by his love of brilliant effects of light.

In England, Tuke settled on the Cornish coast, at Falmouth, where he had spent some of his childhood. He paid occasional visits to Newlyn, and shared with artists there an interest in the busy activities of the fishing community. Stanhope Forbes particularly admired Tuke's work, noting, in a letter to his mother, that "he is now painting this British youth in the style the British matron so strongly objects to". By this he was referring to Tuke's preoccupation with the study of nude boys in the open air–an interest shared with Stott, whose **A Summer Day** was shown at the R.S.B.A. in the winter of 1886-7. These figures were, of course, challenging in many ways. They reflect an enthusiasm for Greek sculpture, and a concern to study the effects of light on the nude–a highly traditional preoccupation. At the same time, there is obviously a fascination for the poignant sensuality of these youthful figures, who are invested with a quality both spiritual and physical. **Two Falmouth Fisher Boys** was first shown in 1885 and again in the following year, at the embryo New English Art Club and it was probably this painting which upset the early backers of the new society. Official success was not too difficult to achieve, however. One of Tuke's most well known paintings, **August Blue**, reflecting the bright light of the Mediterranean, was shown at the Royal Academy in 1894 and purchased by the Chantrey Trustees; it is now in the Tate Gallery.

Tuke was also in considerable demand as a portraitist, and as a painter of what almost might be called 'conversation pieces'. **The Promise**, shown at the N.E.A.C. in 1888 (39) and **The Fisherman** both reveal the characteristic atmosphere of serenity, tinged by the distant threat of nostalgia and even melancholy.

67. The Promise

Oil on canvas, 22 x 26 ins.

The model, Jack Rowling, appeared in several of Tuke's paintings at about this date.

Lent by the Trustees of the National Museums and Galleries on Merseyside, Walker Art Gallery, Liverpool.

68. The Fisherman

Oil on canvas, 44 x 78 ins.

This simple composition, with diagonal lines of oar and fishing line taking the eye to the central figure, was obviously painted from a boat. Tuke started sailing in about 1882, and after this date it became a passion. He frequently painted from one of his boats and, when visiting Tuke in 1887, Stanhope Forbes was entertained on board the 'Julie of Nantes', which housed a large glass studio.

Behind the fisherman in this picture are rowing boat and tall masted ships. A single tug, with smoke staining the sky, acts as

The Lemon Tree (detail)

a reminder of a more hectic world.
Lent by Nottingham Castle Museum.

69. The Lemon Tree

Oil on canvas, 41¼ x 53½ ins.
Lent by the Bradford Art Galleries and Museums.

70. Beach Study

Oil on canvas, 15 x 20½ ins.
Signed and dated lower right. The subject of this evocative little study of 1908 was Charlie Mitchell, one of Tuke's models for many paintings.
Private Collection

George Clausen, 1852-1944

*F*rom his early years, Clausen had a great admiration for Dutch art, with its quiet, domestic themes. He had won a scholarship to the South Kensington Schools, and assisted Edwin Long with the research for his great historical paintings. In 1875, however, he visited the Low Countries and, at the Royal Academy in 1876, he showed a Dutch scene.

The work of Whistler exerted considerable appeal during the late 1870s and, although he later became a pillar of the establishment, Clausen's interest in new ideas, in exploring the qualities of colour and touch, never diminished.

Encouraged by Long, Clausen made his first visit to France. In 1883 he studied at the Académie Julian. By this time, like so many of his contemporaries, Clausen was under the spell of Bastien-Lepage, whom he had met during one of the latter's visits to London. Clausen travelled to Brittany in 1882 and painted **Peasant Girl Carrying a Jar, Quimperlé**–now at the Victoria and Albert Museum–a picture small and decorative in scale, but reflecting much of the intensity of gaze, picturesque appeal, and rich surface facture of Bastien-Lepage's larger works. In 1888, Clausen published a perceptive and persuasive piece on **Bastien Lepage and Modern Realism** in the 'Scottish Art Review'.

Clausen had contacts with many of the radical groups of painters in this country. He was a founder member of the N.E.A.C. as well as a supporter of reform from within the Academy itself. Yet he remained something of an independent, settling to work in the countryside of Hertfordshire, Berkshire, and later, Essex. From 1904-6 he was Professor of Painting at the Academy. His publication of eight lectures he had delivered to his students, **Aims and Ideals in Art**, appeared in 1906. These reveal his emphasis upon individuality; his acute awareness that 'artistic truth' depends upon the artist's context; as well as his respect for tradition.

During the early 1890s, Clausen was under attack for his continued admiration for the Naturalism of Bastien-Lepage. Increasingly, the work of the Impressionists themselves commanded his attention. He studied the paintings of Monet, in particular, and developed a love of brilliant effects of light and colour which continued to inform much of his later work.

71. In the Orchard.

Oil on canvas, 29½ x 19½ins.
This picture was one of the first to reveal the influence of Naturalism. It was painted shortly after Clausen had settled in the countryside, in search of the people and landscape of rural England.
Lent by the City of Salford Art Gallery.

72. An Artist Painting Out of Doors.

Oil on wood, 8¼ x 4¾ins.

This evocative little picture is just one of numerous contemporary images—both paintings and photographs—of artists at work under large, white umbrellas, which served to protect from the elements and to help an even distribution of light.

Lent by the City Museum and Art Gallery, Bristol.

73. Hoeing Turnips.

Watercolour on paper, 14¾ x 20ins.

After a series of delightful orchard pictures, Clausen embarked upon something much more stark. His **Winter Work**, now at the Tate Gallery, was shown at the Grosvenor Gallery in 1883; **Labourers after Dinner** appeared at the Royal Academy in the following year. In 1884 **Hoeing Turnips** was exhibited at the Royal Institute of Painters in Watercolour (610).

This sombre painting attracted considerable attention. It clearly reveals the impact of Millet, with the backs of the workers bent low beneath the horizon; Alfred Sensier's **Jean-François Millet: Peasant and Painter** had appeared in France and England in 1881. 'The Graphic', in particular, responded to this image of rural hard work, praising the "true types of character, robust in form and natural in movement".

(For detailed discussion of Clausen's rustic Naturalism, see Tyne and Wear Museums, **Sir George Clausen R.A., 1852-1944**, catalogue by Kenneth McConkey, 1980.)

Private Collection, courtesy of Pym's Gallery.

74. A Normandy Peasant.

Oil on canvas, 20 x 11¼ins.

Lent by Stoke on Trent Museum and Art Gallery.

75. Souvenir of Marlow Regatta

Oil on wood, 6½ x 9⅝ins.

This delightful little panel painting from 1889 reveals, in its scale and its touch, the continuing influence of the work of Whistler.

Lent by the City Museum and Art Gallery, Leeds.

A Normandy Peasant

Souvenir of Marlow Regatta (detail)

Henry Herbert La Thangue, 1859-1929

*L*ike so many of the artists in this exhibition, La Thangue studied in Paris. He was able to travel to France with a scholarship from the Royal Academy Schools and he worked at the Ecole des Beaux Arts, under Gérôme. His summer trips to Brittany in the early 80s were also important, and in 1882 he exhibited at the Grosvenor Gallery **The Boat Building Yard**, painted at Cancale and directly comparable to **A Street in Brittany** executed by La Thangue's friend Stanhope Forbes, who was working with him in Brittany. Both pictures reveal French influences in the sparkling tonality and interest in the lives of the local people.

La Thangue returned to London in 1884, where he was joined during the following months by a number of British artists hitherto working in Paris, but now perhaps persuaded to leave by the test in the French language, newly imposed by the Ecole des Beaux Arts. Many of these artists had already been considering ways in which they might reform the exhibiting system in Britain. Once back in London, La Thangue was a leading activist in the promotion of such new ideas. When the first N.E.A.C. show was advertised as an "Exhibition of pictures by some of the younger English and American artists whose names are more particularly associated with French methods of study", La Thangue was amongst the participants.

La Thangue, however, felt that the constitution of the N.E.A.C. remained too conservative. He advocated something even more ambitious, with a wider suffrage and, although he lived for much of this time in the remoteness of Norfolk, he remained the leading spirit in the move for a 'National Exhibition'. It was, in the end, an unsuccessful campaign; and yet the determination to encourage a less insular and more democratic approach to training and exhibition in this country certainly had a positive impact.

La Thangue's own painting continued to reveal the influence of French art, particularly that of Bastien-Lepage; although the cool tonality of the Frenchman is replaced by a love of the effects of sunshine and dappled light, as in the engaging **In the Orchard**, shown at the New Gallery in 1893 and now in Bradford Art Gallery. There is also evidence of an interest in the photography of P.H. Emerson, whose images of rural life in Norfolk were widely known. Certainly, the firm, square brush stroke of his earlier work, the confident response to the natural world and the desire also to impose an almost allegorical significance onto his paintings–as in the **Landscape Study** of about 1889–reveal his debt to both France and England.

La Thangue moved from Norfolk at the end of the 1890s, to live in Sussex and he also travelled frequently in Provence, producing pictures such as **A Provençal Spring**, full of light and colour. It was from his village in Petworth that he wrote, in 1905,

Personally I think the painter's life is somewhat akin to the labourer...and has little to interest. He ploughs and sows and the value of his Labour...is only known very many years afterwards.

(Letter dated 7.5.05, in the archives, Oldham Art Gallery.)

In paintings such as **Tucking the Rick**, which was shown at the R.A. in 1902, there is a quality of intensity which reflects some of this deeply felt expression of commitment.

76. A Boatbuilding Yard
Oil on canvas, 30 x 32 ins.
La Thangue had visited Brittany with Stanhope Forbes in the summer of 1881. Both were tackling the problems of working 'en plein air' and it is interesting to compare this bright, compelling picture with Forbes' **A Street in Brittany** (62).
Lent by the National Maritime Museum, Greenwich.

77. Landscape Study
Oil on canvas, 20 x 24 ins.
Painted in Norfolk, in about 1889, the hard reality of rural life is suggested in the dry, sketchy application of the brush, the 'snapshot' view of the back of the figure.
Lent by the Rotherham Metropolitan Borough Council.

78. Portrait of Young Girl
Oil on board, 17 x 12 ins.
Lent by the Towner Art Gallery and Local History Museum, Eastbourne.

79. Tucking the Rick
Oil on canvas, 43 x 35½ ins.
The subtle response to effects of light, the firm, textured brushstroke and the rural theme are characteristic of much of La Thangue's painting. His work was often compared with that of Clausen, who shared his enthusiasms. La Thangue's approach, however, appears more determinedly detached. This, like two other paintings shown at the Royal Academy in 1902, was an

A Boatbuilding Yard

Portrait of Young Girl

image gleaned from the farms around Graffham–La Thangue's home village near Petworth, where picturesqueness is combined with the dominating presence of the dark, north face of the Downs. Three other pictures shown at the R.A. in this year were from Provence; increasingly, the sunlit effects of southern climes became the subject of La Thangue's work,
(See Oldham Art Gallery, **A Painter's Harvest, H.H. La Thangue, 1859-1929,** catalogue by Kenneth McConkey, 1978.)
Lent by Mason, Owen and Partners.

Frederick William Jackson, 1859-1918

Jackson's initial training was not conventional, but he did have early contacts with a group of young artists known as the 'Manchester School', who not only admired the art of the French Barbizon painters, but also worked in Brittany during the 1870s.

In the early 1880s Jackson also crossed the Channel, studying in Paris and painting in the French countryside. It was during these years that William Stott was also working in France; doubtless Jackson paid particular attention to the work of a fellow artist from Oldham and must have seen the two 'plein air' paintings Stott exhibited with such success at the Salon in 1882, **La Baignade** and **Le Passeur** (The Ferry).

Jackson exhibited at the Manchester Academy and the Paris Salon, and he also became a founder member of the N.E.A.C. in 1886. He did not, however, become closely involved with the politics of radical art in London, preferring instead to move to Hinderwell, near Whitby in about 1884. Here, on the wild Yorkshire coast at Staithes, he joined with several other artists, including J.W. Booth and Harold and Laura Knight, painting the landscape and the fishermen, whose lives appear to have been far more rugged than that enjoyed by their peers in Newlyn. Indeed, although Jackson and his colleagues shared the Newlyners' dedication to the ideal of working out of doors in all weathers, their lot was much harsher. Laura Knight described the difficulties, and their consequences, when she wrote of Jackson,

He painted out of doors in any weather. Under the mittens he wore, his hands were swollen, stiff and chapped, as were the edges of his ears and the wings of his nostrils.
(Rochdale Art Gallery, **F.W. Jackson, 'Plein Air' Painter,** catalogue by Michael Cross, 1978).

Conditions were not always so bad, however, and there are many pictures depicting bright warmth and colour, as **In Summer Time**, 1888, or the later **In the Spring Time** of c.1906.

80. Runswick Bay
Oil on canvas, 28 x 43 ins.
Lent by Oldham Art Gallery

81. In the Spring Time
Oil on canvas, 40½ x 80⅝ ins.
This vast, densely painted image of rural life reveals Jackson's interest in colour and light. It also displays something of the taste for decorative effects which must have been encouraged by the work he did with his friend, Edgar Wood, the eminent Arts and Crafts architect and gardener.
Lent by Bradford Art Galleries and Museums.

Runswick Bay (detail)

James Guthrie, 1859-1930

Originally destined to study law, Guthrie's artistic training was somewhat piecemeal in the early years. In the later 1870s he worked in London with the Scottish painter of narrative subjects, John Pettie. During the summers, however, Guthrie soon established a pattern which was to become commonplace amongst the young Glasgow artists, of painting in the countryside, returning to the studio for the winter to work on major exhibition pieces. This fairly conventional approach resulted in success when Guthrie's large **Funeral Service in the Highlands** (now in Glasgow Art Gallery), begun during the summer of 1881 at Brig o' Turk, in the Trossachs, was accepted by the Royal Academy.

The summer of 1882 saw Guthrie working in the flat countryside of Lincolnshire. The brilliantly coloured **To Pastures New** (Aberdeen Art Gallery), with its dramatically simple composition of a young girl and a gaggle of geese, was the result of this sojourn. It seems to represent a sudden and appreciative response to the work of Bastien-Lepage, widely available during this summer in London–when Guthrie's own first work to be included in the Academy was on show.

Of the 'Glasgow School', George Henry, Joseph Crawhall and Edward Walton were particularly close to Guthrie; during the mid 1880s Cockburnspath was the centre of their summer activities. Only Guthrie remained in this small Scottish village during the winter, pursuing his interest in rural subjects.

In the later 1880s, Guthrie began to experiment with pastels, a medium already enjoyed by his compatriots, most notably Crawhall and Walton. Guthrie showed a series of marvellous pastel studies in London and Glasgow in 1890-91 and there is no doubt that working in this technique encouraged him to become more fluent and experimental with his oils. Perhaps disillusioned with his isolation in the countryside, Guthrie had moved back to Glasgow in the mid 1880s. There he had been joined by painters returned from extended periods of study in France–including Alexander Roche and John Lavery. He increasingly moved away from rural themes, concentrating instead on the urban middle classes, celebrating the elegance of their lifestyle with swift, fluent strokes. **Midsummer** portrays the sisters of his fellow painters with a delightful brilliance and ease.

The success of the 'Glasgow School' in London and Munich in 1890 meant that, from this time on, Guthrie was never without a commission for a portrait. These he approached with seriousness, sometimes with the deftness of touch and subtle handling of tone, gleaned from Whistler, whom he admired. He rarely displayed the spontaneity or daring exhibited in his earlier work. By 1903 Guthrie found himself President of the Royal Scottish Academy; he took the opportunity to make Whistler an honorary member of the only British Academy to recognise him.

82. Midsummer

Oil on canvas, 41 x 51 ins.

This brilliant, broadly executed painting of 1892, inscribed lower left James Guthrie, was presented to the Royal Scottish Academy as Guthrie's Diploma work. It stands out in his oeuvre as an experimental piece–a fact he later rather regretted. It is interesting to observe the Scottish artists moving away from a preoccupation with the picturesque lives of the rural worker, and towards the leisured, elegant and enjoyable lives of the middle class.

Lent by the Royal Scottish Academy, Edinburgh.

John Lavery, 1856-1941

John Lavery, who was to become a leading member of the Glasgow School, was actually born in Belfast, but he studied at the Glasgow School of Art and in London in the 1870s, before going to Paris to work in the Académie Julian in 1881.

Lavery's early interest in portrait painting and photography influenced much of his career; nevertheless, his studies in Paris introduced him to the idea of working 'en plein air'. When, in 1883, he discovered the village of Grès, he celebrated the charm and freshness of the landscape and its inhabitants in pictures reminiscent of the work of Bastien-Lepage and of William Stott of Oldham, who was also working in Grès. Lavery achieved early success when his **Les Deux Pêcheurs** was hung in the Salon next to Manet's **Bar at the Folies Bergères** in 1883.

At the Glasgow Institute of 1885, a substantial body of work from the Glasgow School was on show, including Lavery's **On the Loing–An Afternoon Chat**, now at the Ulster Museum, Belfast. Lavery stayed in Glasgow this year, and began to develop his interest in painting stylish images of contemporary middle-class life. Vivid watercolour sketches such as **Woman on a Safety Tricycle** culminated in the luminous **The Tennis Party**, (Aberdeen Art Gallery), which appeared at the Royal Academy in 1886. This picture was also a great success when it was included in the prestigious exhibition at Munich in 1890; it was applauded and purchased by the Bavarian Government.

Woman on a Safety Tricycle (detail)

From this date Lavery's success was assured. In 1888 he had frequented the Glasgow International Exhibition, painting and sketching scenes which were full of lively activity. These, such as **The Musical Ride of the 15th Hussars during the Military Tournament**, **The Flower Show** and **The Glasgow Exhibition**, clearly reveal the impact of the fluent touch, the command of tone, the fascination for the fleeting moment, and the elegant style of Whistler. It comes as no surprise to discover that Lavery had met the 'master' in 1887, had exhibited with him at the R.S.B.A. and had left for the N.E.A.C. with the other 'Artists'.

Like many of the others of the Glasgow School, Lavery moved to London in the 1890s, where he devoted an increasing amount of his time to portraiture. The grand **Lady in Black**, of 1909, reveals the continuing impact of Whistler and it was Lavery who, as Vice-President of the International Society, kept Whistler in constant touch with developments.

83. Woman on a Safety Tricycle

Watercolour, 14 x 20½ ins.

In the summer of 1885, Lavery worked on a series of pictures of the daily life of the elegant, urban middle classes. He reflected the contemporary preoccupation with sport, especially for women. His ladies play tennis, dance and ride their cycles, struggling to manage their elaborate costumes. He worked in both oil and watercolour, capturing the light and mood with delicate precision.

Lent by the Government Art Collection, London.

84. The Flower Show

Oil on canvas, 10½ x 10½ ins.

Lavery spent much of the summer of 1888 at the International Exhibition, making numerous sketches of the crowds and events at the show. About fifty of these were exhibited together at Craibe Angus' Gallery in Queen Street, Glasgow, in October 1888, to considerable popular acclaim.

Lent by Kirkcaldy Museum and Art Gallery.

The Flower Show (detail)

The Musical Ride of the 15th Hussars during the Military Tournament, Glasgow International Exhibition, 1888 (detail)

85. The Musical Ride of the 15th Hussars during the Military Tournament, Glasgow International Exhibition, 1888.
Oil on canvas, 12⅛ x 15 ins.
Lent by the Museum and Art Gallery, Dundee.

86. The Glasgow Exhibition
Oil on wood, 9¼ x 13¾ ins.
One painting of this subject, **At the Glasgow Exhibition**, appeared at the N.E.A.C. in 1889 (40).
Lent by the Trustees of the Tate Gallery, London.

87. The Lady in Black
Oil on canvas, 75 x 36 ins.
If Lavery produced many small sketches and studies of the Glasgow Exhibition, undoubtedly the work which commanded most contemporary attention was the large, commemorative picture of Queen Victoria's visit to the show in August 1888. So successful was this sizeable picture, which included no fewer than 253 individual portraits, that Lavery was henceforth in great demand as a portraitist. **The Lady in Black** is characteristically elegant, revealing all the subtlety of tone and command of composition which originally came from Whistler. It acts as a reminder that in this country 'Impressionism' did not always imply brilliant colour, nor fleeting glimpses of contemporary life.
(See Ulster Museum and Art Gallery, **Sir John Lavery**, catalogue by Kenneth McConkey, 1984).
Lent by the Ulster Museum, Belfast.

References

1. W.P. Frith, **Crazes in Art: Pre-Raphaelitism and Impressionism,** 'Magazine of Art', XI, November 1887–October 1888, p.187.

The Impressionists and their associates were often accused of being diseased, infectious or mad. One of the most virulent examples of such an attack appeared in 1895, when the English translation of Max Nordau's **Degeneration** went through four editions. See p.27:

The curious style of certain recent painters–'impressionists,' 'stipplers,'or 'mosaists,' 'papilloteurs' or 'quiverers,' 'roaring' colourists, dyers in gray and faded tints–becomes at once intelligible to us if we keep in view the researches of the Charcot school into the visual derangements in degeneration and hysteria.

2. Walter Hamilton, **The Aesthetic Movement in England,** London 1882, p.29.

3. Frederick Wedmore, **The Impressionists,** 'Fortnightly Review', January 1883, pp.75-82.

4. D.S. MacColl, **The Logic of Painting,** 'Albemarle Review', September 1892, p.88.

5. Stéphane Mallarmé, **The Impressionists and Edouard Manet,** 'Art Monthly Review', 1876, I, no.9, pp.117-121.

6. As, like you, I believe there is not much chance of doing anything in our stupid country, with its population of bureaucrats, I want to try and arrange for an exhibition in London next year.

Letter from Manet to Fantin Latour, 26 August, 1868. Quoted in Pierre Courthion and Pierre Cailler (eds.), transl. Michael Ross, **Portrait of Manet by Himself and his Contemporaries,** London 1960, p16.

7. John Hollingshead, **The Grasshopper. A Drama in Three Acts. Adapted from 'La Cigale' by MM. Meilhac and Halévy,** London 1887.

When presenting **La Cigale** in Paris in 1877, Meilhac and Halévy lampooned Impressionism in the person of Degas, rather than Whistler.

8. Théodore Duret, **Histoire de Whistler et de son Oeuvre,** Paris 1904, p.65.

9. Review of Fine Art Society exhibition of Whistler's etchings, **The Impressionists and the 'Values' of Nature,** 'Artist', 1 May 1883, iv, p.69.

10. The 'Ten o' clock Lecture' was first delivered in Princes Hall on 20th February, 1885, and was repeated several times in England. Mallarmé translated it into French in 1888 and it was included by Whistler in **The Gentle Art of Making Enemies,** published in 1890.

11. Letter dated 28 February 1883; John Rewald (ed.), **Camille Pissarro. Letters to Lucien,** London 1943, p.22.

12. One verse from **The Sufferings of an Old Suffolk Streeter,** published in 'Fun' and quoted by A. Ludovici, **The Whistlerian Dynasty at Suffolk Street,** 'Art Journal', July 1906, p.195.

13. 'Pall Mall Gazette', 11 June 1888.

14. A.S. Hartrick, **A Painter's Pilgrimage Through Fifty Years,** Cambridge 1939, p.145.

15. W.J. Laidlay, **The Origin and First Two Years of the New English Art Club,** London 1907, p.57.

W.J. Laidlay was very active during the early stages of setting up the N.E.A.C., taking on administrative and financial responsibilities. It is quite clear from his account that he was deeply upset by claims from "a wise man in the East", who declared the aims and ambitions of the Club were "absurdly narrow". This critic was H.H. La Thangue, who longed for the selecting and hanging committee to be elected by "the votes of every artist in the British Isles". The debate aroused many passions and, although La Thangue remained disappointed, his ideas certainly informed the constitution of the N.E.A.C. in some small measure.

16. P.G. Hamerton, 'The Times', 12 April 1886, p.4 This notice of the first show of the N.E.A.C. is quoted by Laidlay, ibid. p.204.

17. Augustus John, **Chiaroscuro: Fragments of Autobiography: First Series,** London 1952, p.48.

18. W.R. Sickert, **The Scotsman,** 24 April 1889.

19. W.R. Sickert, **Impressionism,** 'London Impressionists', The Goupil Gallery, December 1889, p.7.

20. W.R. Sickert, ibid.

21. E. Armitage, **The Impressionists,** 'Athenaeum', 23 July 1887, no.3117, pp.123-4.

22. D.S. MacColl, **Nineteenth Century Art,** London 1902, pp.162-6. MacColl here discusses the work of Monet:

Monet aimed at a stricter truth than Turner, at seizing the momentary balance of values that makes the beauty of an illumination…Monet took his canvas or set of canvases into the open, and limited himself to what he could seize of a particular illumination while it lasted. Out of 'one subject', a haystack, a church, a tree, he made twenty pictures, by discrimination of the successive lights that played upon them.

…the special modern delight in the beauties of aerial tone may be represented as a study of the science of light and colour.

23. On 12th February 1905 Monet wrote to Durand-Ruel from Giverny:

Mais cela signifie pas grand'chose, et que mes cathédrales, mes Londres et autres toiles soient faites d'après nature ou non, cela ne regarde personne et ça n'a aucune importance. Je connais tant de peintres qui peignent d'après nature et ne font que des choses horribles.

Lionello Venturi (ed.) **Les Archives de L'Impressionisme,** New York 1968, Vol.I, p401.

24. In a letter from Stanhope Forbes to his mother, 26 September 1884; quoted by Caroline Fox and Francis Greenacre, **Artists of the Newlyn School, 1800-1900,** Newlyn Orion Galleries 1979, p.59.

25. Letter to Elizabeth Armstrong (Forbes' future wife), undated, ? November 1886:

Gotch has told me much about the Whistler gang lately. I cannot find words strong enough to show my contempt for them.

Caroline Fox and Francis Greenacre, ibid., p.60.

26. See Ronald Pickvance, **A Man of Influence: Alex Reid**, Scottish Arts Council Exhibition, Glasgow 1967.

27. James L. Caw, **A Phase of Scottish Art**, 'Art Journal', 1894, p.75.

28. James L. Caw, ibid.

29. Introduction to R.A.M. Stevenson's, **The Art of Velasquez**, first published in 1895. 1962 edition, with biographical study of the author and textual notes by D. Sutton and T. Crombie, p.44.

30. Ibid., p.160.

31. A. Ludovici was most active in trying to secure several paintings for the exhibition. He wrote to Degas requesting an interview when he was in Paris, but he received a disgruntled letter in return:

J'aurai voulu que votre Président Whistler, mon vieil ami, défendît là ma liberté et m'épargnât cette petite trahison...

A. Ludovici, **An Artist's Life in London and Paris 1870-1925**. London 1926, p.121.

32. See R. Pickvance, **L'Absinthe in England**, 'Apollo', May 1963, p.395.

D.S.MacColl's opening defence of Degas's painting appeared in the 'Spectator', 25 February 1893, lxx, p.256.

33. Camille Mauclair, **Edouard Manet**, 'Art Journal', September 1895, xxxiv, pp.274-9.

34. Frank Rutter, **Art in My Time**, London 1933, p.57.

35. Frank Rutter, ibid., p.101.

36. For Rutter's account of events, see his discussion of the 'Impressionists at the Grafton Gallery', ibid., pp.101-20.

37. Laurence Housman, **Two Kinds of Impressionism**, 'Manchester Guardian', 17 January 1905, p.5.

38. Lady Eastlake, **Letters and Journals**, Vol.II, London 1895, p.159.

39. Camille Mauclair, **The French Impressionists 1860-1900**, 1903, transl. P.G. Konody, p.4.

40. Wynford Dewhurst, **Impressionist Painting: its Genesis and Development**, London 1904, p.4.

Provenances

James McNeill Whistler

1. Nocturne in Black and Gold: The Firewheel.
Bought from Whistler by A. H. Studd 1896, by whom bequeathed to National Gallery 1919; translated to Tate 1949.
Exh: London, Grosvenor 1883 (115) as 'The Great Firewheel'; Munich 1888 (2455); New York 1889 (54); Paris Salon 1890 (2440); London Goupil 1892 (7); Boston 1904 (66); Paris 1905 (65).
Ref: Way and Dennis 'The Art of JMW' London 1903 pp.59-60; Pennell 'The Life of JMW' London & Philadelphia 1908 I p.228; Ludovici 'An Artist's Life in London and Paris' 1926 pp.90-1; Laughton 'Apollo' LXXXVI 1967 p.378; Taylor 'JMW' Cassell 1978 p.73; Young 'The Paintings of JMW' Yale UP 1980 (169) illus.

2. Cliffs and Breakers
Bequeathed by Miss R. Birnie Philip 1958.
Exh: London, Dowdeswell 1884 (37) as 'The Green Headland'; Colnaghi 'Glasgow University's Pictures' 1973 (87); Tokio, Isetan Museum 1987-8 (16).
Ref: Farr 'Burlington Magazine' CXII 1970 p.50; Taylor 'JMW' Cassell 1978 pp.156-7 illus.; Young 'The Paintings of JMW' Yale UP 1980 (278) illus.; Cross 'Painting the Warmth of the Sun' 1984 illus.; Davies 'The St. Ives Years' 1984 p.7.

3. A Shop with a Balcony.
Bequeathed by Miss R. Birnie Philip 1958.
Exh: London & New York 'JMW' 1960 (58); Nottingham 'JMW' 1970 (14) illust.; London, Colnaghi 'Glasgow University's Pictures' 1973 (108); Tokio, Isetan Museum 1987-8 (390).
Ref: Eitner and Fryberger 'Themes and Variations' Stanford University 1978 pp.50, 80; Young 'The Paintings of JMW' Yale UP 1980 (526) illus.

4. Portrait Study of a Man.
London, Redfern; bought Clifford Hall 1940/1; his auction Sotheby's 22.6.55 (139); bought Chandler; Roland, Browse and Delbanco; E. Milner White 1956, by whom bequeathed to Fitzwilliam 1963, received 1970.
Ref: Young 'The Paintings of JMW' Yale UP 1980 (405) illus.

5. Winter Exhibition of the S.B.A.
Signed with artist's device lower left.
G. R. Halkett; purchased for Ashmolean 1943.
Exh: ACGB 1960 (124); Berlin 1969 (127).
Ref: Pennell 'The Whistler Journal' illus. opp. p.177; Taylor 'JMW' Cassell 1987 pp.111-112.

William Stott of Oldham

6. The North Breeze.
Signed lower right William Stott of Oldham.
1938 P. Jones.

8. Woodland Scene Brantrake.
Inscribed lower right 7 William Stott of Oldham.
1967 Fine Art Society.

9. The Artist's Wife.
Signed lower right.

Paul Maitland

16. Factories Bordering the River.
Presented anon. in memory of Terence Rattigan 1983.

18. A House seen through Trees and Shrubs.
Signed lower left.
Bequeathed by Mr. F. F. Madan 1962.
Exh: London Leicester Gall. 'Paul Maitland' 1952 (66); Colnaghi 'Madan Collection' 1962 (20).

19. Kensington Gardens.
Signed lower left.
Bequeathed by Mr. F. F. Madan 1962.

20. Kensington Gardens, Vicinity of the Pond.
Presented C. Andrade 1928.

Theodore Roussel

21. The Bathers.
Exh: Royal Academy 'Post Impressionism' 1979-80 (331) illus.

25. Approaching Storm, Dover.
Signed lower left.
Presented by Miss Herriot 1947.
Exh: ACGB 'Landscape in Britain 1850-1950' 1983 (60) illus.
Ref: Taylor 'James McNeill Whistler' Cassell 1978 p.161.

Walter Richard Sickert

28. Violets.
Signed upper right Sickert.
Mrs. John Lane, by whom given to Bath 1925.
Exh: Bath 'Coronation Exhib. of Flower Paintings' 1953 (41); Sheffield, Graves 1957 (76); London and Edinburgh Fine Art Society 'Sickert' 1973 (4).

29. Clodgy Point, Cornwall.
Inscribed lower right Sickert (?) St. Ives.
Mrs. F. Swanick; Mrs. Holland; Rex NanKivell; Montague Shearman; Mark Oliver; B.C. Adkin; Palmeira Sales, Brighton 1968; Glasgow University 1969.
Ref: Farr 'Burlington Magazine' 112 1970 pp.48-51 illus.; Baron 'Sickert' Phaidon 1973 (19).

30. Dieppe La Plage.
Signed lower right Sickert.
G. Beatson Blair; Manchester 1941.

31. Sea Piece.
Signed lower right.
Sir Hugh Walpole/R.H.Walpole/Edinburgh 1965.
Ref: Dempsey 'Apollo' 83 1966 pp.30-7 illus.; Baron 'Sickert' Phaidon 1973 (29).

32. A Shop in Dieppe.
M. Comiot; University of Glasgow 1955.
Ref: Baron 'Sickert' Phaidon 1973 (30/3).

33. The Red Shop, October Sun.
Exh: Paris Exposition Universelle, British Section 1889 (142); ACGB 'Sickert' 1964 (2); Hull 'Sickert' 1978 p.8; Royal Academy 'Post Impressionism' 1979-80 (336) illus.
Ref: Baron 'Sickert' Phaidon 1973 (110).

34. View of Ramsgate.
Inscribed Sickert pinx.t.
D. W. Hughes & Co.

35. L'Hôtel Royal.
Signed lower right.
Sold by the artist to Arthur Hilton; Agnews 1936; F. R. Duckworth; Agnews; G. Pilkington; Tib Lane Gallery; bought by Hull 1960.
Exh: ACGB 'Sickert' 1964 (6); ACGB 'Decade 1890-1900' 1967 (38); Hull 'Sickert in the North' 1968 (9); London Fine Art Society 'Sickert' 1973 (20); Dundee 'English Painting' 1979 (1); ACGB 'The Nature of Painting' I. Light, Sheffield (38); Humphrey Ocean touring exhib. 1986-7 illus.
Ref: R. Emmons, 'Life and Opinions of W.R.S.' 1941, p.113; Ferens Art Gall. Bull. Jan. 1961; W. Baron 'Sickert' Phaidon 1973 (110) illus.
The Hôtel Royal in Dieppe was a favourite subject for Sickert before it was demolished in 1900.

36. St. Mark's Facade, Venice.
Signed lower right.
Bequeathed by Mr. Montague Shearman through Contemporary Art Society 1940.
Exh: London Redfern Gallery 'Sherman Collection' 1940 (16); Hove 'Sickert' 1950 (16); Folkestone '19th century English Art' 1965.
Ref: Browse 'Sickert' 1960 p.107 (1); Baron 'Sickert' Phaidon 1973 (81) illust.

37. The Theatre of the Young Artist.
Inscribed lower left Sickert Dieppe 1890.
Exh: Sheffield, Graves 'Sickert' 1957 (7); ACGB 'Decade 1890-1900' 1967 (30); N. Ireland, Londonderry Gwyns Inst. 1967; Folkestone 1972; Eastbourne, Towner 'Sickert in Dieppe' 1975; Guildford 1975; ACGB 'Sickert' 1977-8 (4); Southport, Atkinson A.G. 'Victorian Centenary Exhib.' 1978-9; Australia, Brisbane and Nat. Gall. of Victoria 1979.
Ref: Baron 'Sickert' Phaidon 1973 (64) illus.

38. Minnie Cunningham at the Old Bedford.
Signed lower right W. Sickert.

Ref: Baron 'Sickert' Phaidon 1973 (46) illus.

39. George Moore.
Signed lower left Sickert.
Bought by P.W. Steer from artist 1910; Tate 1917.
Exh: Tate 'Paintings and Drawings' 1960 (13); Australia, Adelaide 'Sickert' 1968 (7).
Ref: Moore 'Speaker' 20.2.92; Baron 'Sickert' Phaidon 1973 (55) illus.

40. The Gallery at the Old Bedford.
Signed Sickert.
Paris, Hotel Drouôt sale 1909 (8); Adolphe Tavernier; Contesse Solcedo de Rios; a French dealer; Adams Gallery: purchased from the Mayor Galleries 1947.
Exh: Bernheim-Jeune 1907 (22); Glasgow 1937.
Ref: Baron 'Sickert' Phaidon 1973 (73) illus.

41. Noctes Ambrosianae.
Signed lower right Sickert.
Walter Taylor; J. B. Priestley; Nottingham 1952.
Exh: Salon d'Automne 1906 (1545); Tate 'Paintings and Drawings' 1960 (18); ACGB 'Sickert' 1964 (14).
Ref: Dimson 'Burlington Mag.' 102 1960 pp.438-43 illus.; Baron 'Sickert' Phaidon 1973 (230) illus.

Philip Wilson Steer

43. Surf.
Signed lower left P. W. Steer.
Anon. sale Christie's 1910, 1918, 1919; F. Hindley Smith, by whom bequeathed to Fitzwilliam Museum 1939.
Exh: ACGB 1960 (7); Cambridge, Fitzwilliam 'Philip Wilson Steer' 1986 (2).
Ref: MacColl 'Life, Work and Setting' p.190; Laughton 'PWS', OUP 1971 (16) illus.

44. Figures on the Beach at Walberswick.
Steer; Christie's 1942 (147); B. H.; H. J. Paterson; Nicholson; Humphrey Brooke; Tate 1947.
Ref: Laughton 'PWS' OUP 1971 (54).

45. The Beach at Walberswick.
Geo. Healing; Tate 1942.
Ref: Laughton 'PWS' OUP 1971 (55).

46. Girls Running, Walberswick Pier.
Inscribed lower right Steer 94.
Sir Augustus Daniel; presented to Tate Gallery by Lady Daniel 1951.
Exh: London Goupil Gallery 'Steer' 1894 (37) as 'Girls Running'; London Goupil Gallery 'Representative work by some of the Foremost Painters' 1921 (3) as 'Girls on the Pier'; London Barbizon House 1927 (26) as 'Walberswick Pier'; Paris British Council 'British Painting' 1938; London Leicester Galleries 'The Collection of the Late Sir Augustus Daniel' 1951 (86); Cambridge, Fitzwilliam 'Philip Wilson Steer' 1986 (10) illus.
Ref: 'Spectator' 17.3.94 p.373; Ironside 'Wilson Steer' Phaidon 1943 pl.24; MacColl 'Life, and Setting of PWS' London 1945 pp.49,195; Laughton 'Apollo' 1970 pp.212-214; Laughton 'PWS' OUP 1971 (68).

47. Two Girls on Walberswick Beach.
Oil on wood, 25.4 x 35.6cm.
Major J. A. Hamilton; Christie's 25.8.58 (42); Agnew's, from whom bought by Plymouth, 1960.
Exh: Cambridge, Fitzwilliam 'Philip Wilson Steer' 1986 (7).
Ref: Laughton 'Apollo' 1985, p.405; Laughton 'PWS' OUP 1971 (43).

49. The Sprigged Frock.
Moffat Lindner: Barbizon House; Sir Frank Brangwyn; by whom presented in 1955.
Exh: London, Grosvenor, Society of British Pastellists 1890 (129); Brussels Les XX Feb. 1891 (Steer no.1); ACGB 'Decade 1890-1900' 1966-7 (41); Cambridge, Fitzwilliam 'PWS' 1986 (13) illus.
Ref: Laughton 'PWS' OUP 1971 (70) illus.

50. A Young Girl in a White Dress.
Signed upper right Steer 92.
C. A. Jackson of Manchester; G. Beatson Blair; bequeathed to Manchester 1941.

Exh: ?Goupil Gallery 1894 (33) as 'Little Girl with a Pink Sash'; Birkenhead, Williamson 'Philip Wilson Steer' 1951 (8); Gloucester 'P. Wilson Steer' 1959 (7); London & New York, Noortman & Brod 'Some Masterpieces from the Manchester City A.G.' 1983 (26); Cambridge, Fitzwilliam 1986 (17) illus.
Ref: MacColl 'Life, Work and setting of PWS' London 1945 p.193; Laughton 'PWS' OUP 1971 (101).

Sidney Starr
52. Miss Gertrude Kingston.
Ref: McConkey 'Edwardian Portraits' Antique Collectors' Club 1987 p.89 illus.

William L. Wyllie
55. The Thames near Charing Cross.
Gift of the Family of Mr and Mrs Thomas Parker, in their memory.
Exh: 1986 NEAC Centenary at Christies, Cat. No. 110, Illus. p72.

56. Romney Marsh.
Oscroft Bequest.

Francis Bate
57. The Weeping Ash
Presented by the artist 1911
Exh: Grosvenor Gallery, New English Art Club, The London Impressionists, 1889.

Arthur Studd
58. Washing Day.
Roland, Browse and Delbanco; bought E. Milner White 1955; by whom given to York 1958.
Exh: Roland, Browse and Delbanco 1955 (32).

59. Venetian Twilight.
Roland, Browse and Delbanco; bought E. Milner White; by whom given to York 1958.

60. A Venetian Lyric.
Presented Mrs. F. Gibson 1918.

Stanhope Forbes
61. A Street in Brittany.
Purchased from the artist at Autumn Exhibition 1882.
Exh: Royal Academy 1882 (104); Walker, Liverpool Autumn 1882 (464); Plymouth 1923 (35); N.E.A.C. 'Retrospective' 1924; Manchester 1925; 'Artists of the Newlyn School' 1958 (9); Plymouth 'Stanhope A. Forbes' 1964 (1); Newlyn Orion 'Artists of the Newlyn School' 1979 (1); Royal Academy 'Post Impressionism' 1979-80 (288) illus.
Ref: 'Art Journal' 1892 p.45; 'Scribner's Magazine' June 1894 pp.688-90; 'Strand Magazine' 1901 p.492; 'Art Journal' Christmas 1911; Wortley 'British Impressionism' 1988 p.85 illus.

62. Evening, Workers Return.
Donated by Sir William Cresswell Gray, Hartlepool.

63. Gala Day at Newlyn.
Donated by Sir William Cresswell Gray, Hartlepool.
Exh: "Painting in Newlyn" 1985 Newlyn Orion Gallery, Barbican Art Gallery; "The Edwardian Era" 1987 Barbican Art Gallery.

Thomas Cooper Gotch
64. The Estuary, Etaples.
Signed lower right T. C. Gotch.
Presented by M. Berrill 1967.
Exh: Newlyn Orion 'Artists of the Newlyn School' 1979 (58).

65. The Silver Hour.
Signed lower right T. C. Gotch.
Acquired after the artist's Memorial Exhibition, Kettering, 1932.
Exh: Kettering 'Memorial Exhib.' 1932; Newlyn Orion 'Artists of the Newlyn School' 1979 (66); London, Barbican 'Painting at Newlyn' 1985.

William Holt Yates Titcomb
66. Old Sea Dogs.
Exh: 1903 Whitechapel Art Gallery; 1983 Watford "Herkomer Students" exhibition; 1985 Bushey Museum Trust, W.H.Titcomb exhibition. ACGB 1960 (124); Berlin 1969 (127).

Henry Scott Tuke
67. The Promise.
Signed H. S. Tuke 1888.
Bought from N.E.A.C. by Percy Arden; his sale Christie's; Sampson 1909; Kennedy 1911; George Audley, by whom presented to the Walker 1925.
Exh: N.E.A.C. 1888 (39); Walker, Liverpool, Autumn Exhib. 1924 (874); Hanley 1929; Falmouth 'Tuke Centenary' 1957; 'Artists of the Newlyn School' 1958 (54); Newlyn Orion 'Artists of the Newlyn School' 1979 (43), illus.
Ref: 'Portfolio' 1888 p.104; 'Windsor Magazine' I 1895 p.608, illus.; 'Athenaeum' 26.3.10 p.371.

68. The Fisherman.
Purchased from exhibition of works of Cornish painters 1894.
Exh: Grosvenor Gallery 1889; Tuke Centenary Exhibition, Falmouth, 1958; Tuke Exhibition, Usher Art Gallery, Lincoln.
Ref: 1985, Wainwright and Dinn, Sarema Press.

69. The Lemon Tree.
Inscribed lower right H. S. Tuke 1893(5?).
Bought from the artist 1898.
Exh: Munich 1894; Bradford 'English Impressions' 1978 (46).
Ref: 'Magazine of Art' 1902; Wainwright and Dinn 'H.S.T. Under Canvas' Sarema Press 1989 illus. p.58 as 'A Corfu Garden'.

George Clausen
71. In the Orchard.
Inscribed lower left G. Clausen 1881.
W. Smith, from whose estate bought by Salford 1948.
Exh: Tyne and Wear Museums 'Sir George Clausen' 1980 (23a) illus.

72. An Artist Painting Out of Doors.
Inscribed G. Clausen 1882.
Hugh Clausen (son of the artist), by whom given to Bristol 1949.
Exh: Tyne and Wear Museums 'Sir George Clausen' 1980 (23) illust.; 'Landscape in Britain 1850-1950' 1983 (66).

73. Hoeing Turnips.
Inscribed lower left G. Clausen 1883.
J. S. Hill n.d.
Exh: Paris Exposition Universelle, British Section 1889 (196) as 'Laboureurs'; London Pym's Gallery 'Rural and Utopian Images' 1984 (14).
Ref: 'The Art Journal' 1884 p.191; 'The Graphic' 3.5.84 p.427; 'The Illustrated London News' 3.5.84 p.422 illus.; Magazine of Art 1884 p.446 illus.; 'The Times' 7.5.84 p.6.

74. A Normandy Peasant.
Inscribed lower left G. Clausen 87(?).
Mrs. J. B. Ashwell, by whom given to the city 1949.
Exh: Tyne & Wear Museums 'Sir George Clausen' 1980.

75. Souvenir of Marlow Regatta.
Inscribed on reverse Souvenir of/Marlow Regatta/ G. Clausen.
Sam Wilson, by whom bequeathed to Leeds 1915.

Henry Herbert La Thangue
76. A Boatbuilding Yard.
Signed upper left H.H. La Thangue.
Exh: Grosvenor Gall. 1882.
Ref: Oldham 'A Painter's Harvest' 1978 p.8 illus.; Wortley 'British Impressionism' 1988 p.69 illus.

77. Landscape Study.
Signed lower right H. H. La Thangue.
The gift of E. Nightingale?
Exh: Oldham, 'A Painter's Harvest' 1978 (9) illus.

79. Tucking the Rick.
Signed lower right H. H. La Thangue.
Thomas Agnew n.d.; by 1906 T. F. Blackwell; R.E. Abbott 1942; Sotheby's 25.6.1980 (45) to Pym's Gallery; purchased 1980.
Exh: R.A. 1902 (167); St. Louis International 1904 (75); Newcastle upon Tyne Polytechnic 'Peasantries' 1981 (53) illus.
Ref: 'The Academy' 10.5.02 p.488; 'The Athenaeum' 24.5.02 p.665; 'The Magazine of Art' 1902 p.398; 'The Times' 3.5.02 p.16; 'Spectator' 17.5.02 p.767; 'The Magazine of Art' 1904 p.6.

Frederick William Jackson
80. Runswick Bay.
Signed lower left F. W. Jackson.
Presented by Mrs. Walker Maw 1937.
Exh: Manchester Jackson Memorial 1918; Rochdale 'F. W. Jackson' 1978 (29).

81. In the Spring Time.
Bought from the artist in 1906.
Exh: Manchester Jackson Memorial 1918; Bradford 'English Impressions' 1978 (23); Rochdale 'F. W. Jackson' 1979 (3).

John Lavery
83. Woman on a Safety Tricycle.
Inscribed lower right J. Lavery 1885.
The Frank Gallery, from whom bought 1966.
Exh: The Fine Art Society, Edinburgh and London, Belfast, Dublin 'Sir John Lavery' 1984-5 illus.; The Fine Art Society London and Glasgow 'Pastels and Watercolours by the Glasgow Boys' 1985.

84. The Flower Show.
Signed lower right J. Lavery.
Provost Wilson Kirkcaldy 1958.
Exh: London, Royal Academy 'Post Impressionism' 1979/80 (318).